Advance pra
Home Econ

'Hilarious, audacious, and deeply felt. An idiosyncratic hymn to the drudgery of life!'

—*Sara Baume*

A remarkable piece of writing . . . There is something quietly bracing in encountering such a lucid account of a writing life, one that refuses myth-making while still allowing space for ambition, desire and joy . . . This is a generous, intelligent and finely wrought book.

—*Patrick Holloway*

This is absolutely one to read about the reality of 'making it' as an artist, and how to live, make money and create.

—*The Journal.ie*

Here is the work of the invisible hands that clean buildings in the early hours, soothe babies in the small hours, write books in the zero hours left to them, hands which never down tools no matter how tired they are. A round of applause for these hands. The world would stop turning without them. An illuminating, enlightening read from an illuminating, enlightening writer.

—*Claire Kilroy*

A smart, sad, funny portrait of the artist in delightfully well-crafted prose.

—*Sarah Moss*

I really loved this book . . . in ways that I didn't expect. Caitríona's writing is as sharp and meticulous as her task execution. She brings a depth of introspection and her reflections contain rich political and philosophical thought.

—*Lynn Ruane*

I too work a manual job that pays a pittance, yet still provides more income than writing books. In the end it was Lally's wit, her ever-curious and amused outlook on the daily trials and joys of life, that had me hooked. This book has that delicate quality of seeming simple while containing all the complexity of trying not simply to make a living, but to live.

—*Lucy Sweeney Byrne*

Also by Caitríona Lally

Eggshells
Wunderland

Home Economics

HOME ECONOMICS
First published in 2026 by
New Island Books
Glenshesk House
10 Richview Office Park
Clonskeagh
Dublin D14 V8C4
Republic of Ireland
newisland.ie

Print ISBN: 978-1-83594-035-8
eBook ISBN: 978-1-83594-036-5

British Library Cataloguing in Publication Data. A CIP catalogue record for this book is available from the British Library.

Product safety queries can be addressed to New Island Books at the above postal address or at info@newisland.ie.

Set in 11.25 pt on 16.5 pt Sabon
Typeset by JVR Creative India
Cover design by Sarah McCoy, @sarahmccoy_design
Printed by L&C Printing Group, Poland, lcprinting.eu

the arts council an chomhairle ealaíon funding literature

MIX
Paper | Supporting responsible forestry
FSC www.fsc.org
FSC® C152082

New Island received financial assistance from The Arts Council (An Chomhairle Ealaíon), Dublin, Ireland.

New Island Books is a member of Publishing Ireland and the Independent Publishers Guild.

10 9 8 7 6 5 4 3 2 1

Home Economics

a memoir

Caitríona Lally

NEW ISLAND

For Brian, Alice and Joe

Introduction

This is a book about trying to write a book, a book about a book called *Wunderland*. I wrote it to figure out why I struggled to finish my second novel after the uncomplicated pleasure of writing the first. I wrote it for the same reason I don't teach creative writing; I haven't yet worked out the how and the why. I started writing *Wunderland* in 2014 and it was published in 2021. My focus here is on those seven years, during which I published one book and wrote the second, began work as a cleaner and gave birth to two children, attempting to make these varied strands of my life work together. Nobody can do all of the things all of the time and this book is a muddle of plate-spinning, ball-dropping and other mixed metaphors of a busy time.

Thinking back on those challenging years, with both children now ensconced in school and often sleeping through the night, I wonder at the sheer drive it took to finish *Wunderland*, even as I thought I wasn't measuring up. I can look back with compassion at this addled woman rushing hither and tither and think, *Go easy on yourself, take it handy*. While avoiding that most irritating of new-parent platitudes, *Enjoy every minute*.

This isn't a comprehensive account of those years. It's a series of thoughts and incidents, the timeline often gleaned from old emails and files on my laptop. Gaps and omissions, rememberings, misrememberings and forgettings form this hodgepodge of a memoir.

I'm slightly uneasy about the insistent 'I, I, I' of memoir, thinking of Neil Genzlinger's assertion that unremarkable lives should go unremarked upon, the way God intended. But surely we're all unremarkable in our own way and it's that very unremarkableness that makes us remarkable.

IT'S MARCH 2015 AND I'M BETWEEN JOBS. MY DEBUT novel, *Eggshells*, will be published in a couple of months but I need some kind of paid work to go alongside what will hopefully be a writing career.

When I was a student in Trinity College Dublin in the early 2000s, I spent a couple of summers working in its housekeeping department. I stayed in touch with some of the cleaners, and they tell me that Trinity is hiring housekeeping staff again, after a recession freeze. I apply and am interviewed by the same woman who interviewed me fifteen years earlier. She asks why I want to work there again, saying, Nobody ever comes back. She looks doubtful but agrees to take me on. At least you know how rough the early mornings are, she says, some new recruits don't last the week.

I start the cleaning job the following week, leaving home at 5.25 a.m. to trudge two miles through snow-slush to work, wondering if I've made the right decision.

On the first day I'm introduced to my supervisor, given two blue cleaning smocks with deep pockets for keys and dust cloths and doorstoppers, and brought to the housekeepers' kitchen in the basement of the arts block to meet the other cleaners. (I recognise some of the women from when I attended lectures there; others I've worked with in my student days. It's a mark of the place that many stay for decades, putting the guts of a working life into Trinity's Housekeeping Department.) I, however, am set to work as a spare. If no one is sick or skiving, spares are put doing heavy-duty cleaning tasks that are either not in the duties of a specific cleaner or left undone by a cleaner for reasons of idleness, mutiny, or physical incapability. These tasks include dusting and scrubbing areas that don't get daily or weekly cleans, scraping the chewing gum off the underside of desks in libraries, polishing library balustrades, windows and high window ledges, taking down library books and thoroughly cleaning the shelves. The brief is to clean only as high as you can reach; I'm fairly tall so I clean more shelves than most women and fewer shelves than some men.

Any given day could involve cleaning the stairwells in the arts block, sweeping down the tumbleweedy dustballs and hair clumps before mopping. The stairwells are cosy, enclosed little worlds shut off from the rest of the arts block by heavy fire doors. Students and lecturers who come in early up freshly washed stairs either grimace apologetically and tread lightly, taking two steps at a time to lessen their footprint, or pretend not to see the cleaner or bucket and saunter past as normal. I try not to wish a painful fall on the latter. We're warned, repeatedly, Put out your signs! If you're ever washing a floor you have to put out the yellow Caution Wet Floor sign or else the college won't be covered if there's a fall and a compo claim. I put the signs at the top and bottom of the stairwell as I clean. Various cleaners' names are markered on the signs, often unconnected to whose cubby they're in now; either women long retired or migrated to different areas.

A cleaner's cubby contains her cleaning supplies. Most are the size of a wardrobe, some are walk-in, or even lie-in as a long-deceased cleaner used to do, a legend in the housekeeping community who used to so whole-heartedly enjoy her nightly nights out that she'd curl up under a coat in her cubby, pull shut the door, and sleep off the excess in Cif-smelling darkness. Cleaning accoutrements stored in cubbies include bin bags of various sizes and colours, mops, sweeping brushes, vacuum cleaners, cloths, rags, sponges, rubber gloves, and cleaning creams, sprays, liquids, waxes, powders and ointments. Our cubbies also contain photos of our families; some have religious medals or prayers, pictures of once-attractive celebrities, printouts of jokes about menopause, deodorant, make-up, mugs for sneaky coffees.

Trinity College Housekeeping – now under the banner of Estates & Facilities alongside maintenance workers, security guards, attendants, waste management, postmen and groundsmen – is managed by a small number of supervisors. As a spare, I'm constantly checking in with my supervisor: where am I going today, who am I working with, what keys do I collect from the security desk, what needs to be done, is it a deep clean or a daily servicing? Spare work is exciting in the beginning but after a few months, most spares just want their own area. (A cleaner's area is the place she cleans; areas have long ago been divided up according to space measurement and busyness or frequency of cleaning required.) If a cleaner leaves and is not replaced, her area can be split among co-workers on her floor, extra square footage that can cause ructions unless overtime is given to accommodate the extra work. In order to get my own area, another cleaner must leave (most of the Irish are lifers, the young Brazilians on travel adventures are more transitory), retire (the most common, the Irish women are of that generation), go on long-term sick leave or maternity leave (very uncommon: the Irish cleaners are mostly grandmothers, the cleaners from other countries just passing through are too young and busy studying to be thinking about babies).

Seeing so many different parts of the college with nobody else around feels like sneaking downstairs as a child when your parents are asleep. The rhythms of the college are different in the early morning. You see the secret servants' staircases (in the provost's house), the secret tunnels (connecting the arts block and Long Room Library) and the small, almost-hidden doors of cubbyholes used to store cleaning supplies. Much of the college is in darkness at this time; the cleaners are the ones turning on lights and unlocking doors. It's a topsy-turvy world: doors that are locked during normal hours are open in the early hours; doors that are open during normal hours are locked in the early hours. I rush through the offices; I prefer cleaning lecture rooms with enormous maps or geology specimens, old libraries with comically dull book titles, display cases containing precious manuscripts, which I polish extra slowly.

A motherly cleaner offers advice when I start working as a spare: Never carry a story. Don't become known for bringing gossip from building to building. Gossip and rumour spread like warts in the college, which at times feels like a large, unwieldy family: there are mothers and sons, husbands and wives, aunts and nieces among cleaners, security guards, maintenance crew and office staff. Some go back generations of Trinity workers, and misdemeanours are remembered, grudges and grievances stored, loyalties maintained. I've heard rumours both plausible and outlandish, mostly misunderstandings that have grown legs with each retelling. A rumour starts that a certain cleaner is going for a supervisor's job because she's seen using a computer: there's no truth to it, there seldom is. It's hard to trace them back to remarks misheard or misunderstood or additional detail tacked on for a bit of gas.

As a spare, you learn not to do too good a job on someone else's patch. It can annoy the person you're covering, show them up for what they might not be doing on a regular basis, and result in additional tasks expected of the cleaner. And, it's the easiest thing to be the hero doing extra jobs for a week: long-term work is the real slog.

At the end of my first week I'm exhausted. My body doesn't know if it's coming or going, awake or asleep. My appetite rages out of control: already a fan of junk food, I get a ravenous hunger and eat all around me; being up so early adds at least one extra meal, plus snack, to my day.

When I worked as a student-cleaner in Trinity Housekeeping in 2003 and 2004, I spring-cleaned student accommodation after it was vacated, and then serviced these rooms for summer guests. Spring cleaning was tough work. Some bathrooms hadn't been cleaned for the nine months they were inhabited by students. We weren't allowed to use bleach after a mysterious incident years ago: one rumour had it that a cleaner accidentally drank another cleaner's bleach from a 7Up bottle; another rumour had a cleaner mixing bleach with other cleaning chemicals in an airless shower cubicle and fainting: the truth might be all or none of these things. We were given cream cleaner and snuck in bleach: a stiff nail brush with neat bleach is the only thing that will go near cleaning black, mouldy grouting, even if it had us coughing and spluttering, eyes streaming. Cleaning the bedrooms was easier; the items discovered behind beds weren't always pleasant but occasionally we found decent clothes and a cleaner to fit them, I got a working stethoscope left behind by a medical student. This was the early 2000s, the glitter era; female students' bedrooms had a year's worth of tiny sparkles to dig out with the hoover.

The first summer I cleaned old rooms near the tennis courts in the front of the college. The skips (experienced cleaners in charge of houses) I worked under insisted on opening up the bedrooms before us student cleaners got there, after guests had checked out. They told us it was to remove the worst of the rubbish but it was really to pocket any tips before we caught sight of them. (Since then, I've tried to put cash tips directly into hotel cleaners' hands, mindful of grabby skips and sneaky supervisors.)

The second summer I cleaned old rooms with wooden steps leading up to them near the medical centre. We had our breaks in a cubby the size of a large toilet cubicle, skips and helpers crammed together on rickety stools, knees touching: it was obvious if someone had eaten garlic the night before. The two skips I worked with were kind, very kind, and I'm still friends with them decades later. They kept a tip jar and we pooled the money: I got a pair of boots with my share of the takings. There were plenty of characters in the housekeeping department then. One cleaner played a Peig Sayers-level of poor mouth in front of American tourists, hamming up her health woes and cleaning up on tips: she stopped just short of keening a lament. Another acted as a middle-woman for a son who mysteriously came into apparently high-end goods at knockdown prices.

One morning we sprayed a guest's expensive perfume while cleaning her bathroom, sniffing each other's necks, when she walked in. There was no hiding the smell – we sheepishly scuttled out in a silent cloud of musky jasmine. Another guest had a complicated-looking piece of exercise equipment that the skip and I decided to try out. I helped her onto the floor and arranged her into the device while she rocked herself to and fro, saying by the time she got up she'd be the size of Kate Moss. When we heard footsteps on the stairs I tried to yank her out of the contraption but in the confusion she pulled me down beside her and there we were in a tangled heap, laughing so much we couldn't get up when the guest walked in, unamused.

A CLEANER'S SHIFT STARTS AT 6 A.M. AND FINISHES AT 9.30 a.m., unless we do overtime. I eat a bowl of porridge at home at 5 a.m.; then after work, I have a flask of coffee and second breakfast of a ham sandwich (channelling my farmer uncle's meal after milking is done) on the bench outside the National Library, star-spotting politicians in the adjacent Leinster House grounds, trying not to heckle the worst of them. Then I go to the reading room in the library and write for as long as my brain will stay awake. I sometimes see writers working there – Anne Enright sat a few rows ahead of me one day and I strained, oh how I strained to see what she was at on her laptop, as if some kind of literary seepage were possible and I could make sentences like hers.

If I'm more tired than usual, I go home to nap and then do some writing when I wake. It's coming near publication time, and I've been asked to write some promotional pieces about writing my first novel. I'm unused to writing anything that isn't fiction, and I spend far too long on it, overthinking every word. A month into the cleaning job, I should also be working on my second novel, tentatively titled 'Wunderland'. I began writing it in 2014, shortly after finishing my first novel, with the basic premise of a sister and brother meeting after some time apart. There is a joy in the starting of a project that can be difficult to maintain. I have no publishing deal or deadline for this second novel, it feels very hypothetical. When overtime work is available in Trinity, I take the hours, prioritising the ready money from cleaning over the long-term writing goal. Exhaustion from physical work can be a useful excuse for not writing.

In 2007, after working in Japan and then some dithering around Asia, I got my first full-time job in a publishing company in Dublin, I joyously ensconced myself reading and writing summaries of magazine articles for library users in the United States. But in 2011 I was made redundant. I was devastated. I'd been in the job almost five years and saw myself coasting contentedly to retirement, learning small amounts of information about lots of things: aviation, atomic science, teen lifestyle, politics, baseball, art, business. I also wrote an entire 250-word abstract about a jazz musician I referred to as the Duke of Ellington before discovering it was Duke Ellington.

After being made redundant I spent a year on the dole, queuing defeatedly outside the job centre to sign on while a local drug dealer conducted business transactions loudly on his phone, leaning against his high-spec BMW before sauntering to the top of the queue. I applied unsuccessfully for over 300 jobs in housekeeping, hotel and catering, admin, data entry, customer service, publishing. (Years later, I read that Claire Keegan applied for 300 jobs in a previous recession; 300 must be the magic number for writers.) I carried out an online test for a cleaning job in a five-star hotel, which had photos of bedrooms and corridors accompanied by questions about what was dirty or out of place in the picture; I never got called to interview. I applied for a cleaning job in a hotel that paid minimum wage, which was €8.65 an hour at the time. I got to interview stage and was told I was only guaranteed eight hours per week. I couldn't afford to give up the dole for that huge a drop in income: €188 versus €69.20 (and that's before bus fares are taken into account).

I did an evening creative-writing course. I submitted short stories and essays into various journals but got rejections or silence. I gave up on trying to get published and started writing bits and pieces in a notebook that would eventually become my first novel, *Eggshells*. In 2012, I got a minimum-wage job in data entry. It was stress-free and worked well with my attempts to write my novel on the side. But six months in, a position came up for a better-paid writing position, which involved writing content (content, a dread-word so empty and devoid of meaning) for a US price-comparison website. I had to write the kind of words that encouraged shoppers to buy more superfluous crap they didn't need, I had to use words that pretended a bargain that just wasn't there: 'Up to 75% off' can mean most sale items have 10 per cent off except for one item (a bikini in winter, in sizes XXXS and XXXL only) that's marked 75 per cent off. Likewise, prices 'from' $5 can mean just one item costs $5 while everything else is exponentially more expensive. I found it easy to come up with synonyms for Biggest! Brightest! Best! but I found it bleakly underhanded to use my writing skills to persuade shoppers to buy more useless tat, and I quit, trying to stave off panicky qualms about willingly giving up a job after being unwillingly unemployed for so long.

I enter the first few chapters of my novel into the Irish Writers Centre Novel Fair, and in 2014, I win a place. I get the phone call on a Friday and am told to submit a completed manuscript by the following Monday. I go to Neary's pub for celebratory pints with friends. My partner is away for the weekend: I order enough Chinese food for several days and sit at the kitchen table surrounded by takeaway cartons and cruddy cereal bowls, snipping and shaping my manuscript into submittable form.

The novel fair is a huge thrill. The twelve winning writers sit while agents and publishers move from table to table, at the ring of a bell. I have to explain my writing in a way I haven't yet explained it to myself. I find this part much harder than the actual writing – the attempt to sell my words in a pithy elevator-pitch way is both exhilarating and exhausting. In the weeks and months after the novel fair, rejections trickle in until I get accepted by an agent and a publisher. I feel hope and glee at my entrance into this completely unknown world.

While working as a spare, I get to clean many different parts of the college either on my own or working alongside different cleaners. One sunny morning I'm put cleaning the fourth-floor glass balustrade of the Ussher Library atrium, which wraps around the book area and reading area. Cleaning the inside is fine, but leaning over to clean the outside gives me the belly-swoops, looking straight down the sheer drop to the basement. While I'm polishing the glass, my supervisor rings, hissing quickly down the phone that her boss is coming looking for me: 'make sure to be caught working'. When this boss arrives, she finds me on the phone to the supervisor who's warning me to not be caught dossing.

I clean various floors of the Ussher Library, hoovering the mean red carpets that are reluctant to let go of dirt – luckily the lighting is low. I wipe the desks, which are at odd slant angles, making it particularly difficult to keep in mind which rows I've done or not done. I remember the last-minute studying I did here before my final exams, and pity the students here now in a panic of books and energy drinks. The Ussher is a 24-hour library so we're always cleaning around students and their detritus and irritation at our botherings. There's often a sleeping student pulling an all-nighter whose head shoots up from the desk at the sudden noise of the hoover. The windows face east, the sunrises a joy to watch, the trees pressing into the glass (I imagine Moonface and Saucepan Man in *The Magic Faraway Tree* clambering up into the Land of Books). The library toilets are busy, always busy. There are beard-trimmings (I hope) in the men's wash-hand basins, make-up smears in the women's. I sweep up food wrappers in the women's toilets and pull out sandwich wrappers, McDonald's paper bags and curry cartons from behind toilet cisterns: whether shame of being seen to eat or shame of eating alone or shame of eating itself is the reason, it saddens me.

I work alongside some of the women who clean floors of the arts block. Getting to know them becomes my favourite part of the job; their lives and their different cleaning methods. Most attack the toilets first, get the biggest job out of the way, but some start with offices to ease themselves in. There are tough lives graciously lived: the far-reaching effects of addiction, homeless daughters and sons living in hotel rooms on waiting lists for social housing, paying off loved ones' drug debts and child maintenance; dogged overtime worked to put kids through college or send back to family in other countries. I have small first-world worries – how will my book be received, will it sell many copies? – and these larger worries makes me think of the phrase, Check your privilege.

I remember a cleaner describing her husband's illness and the stress of losing his income, saying, How to not get bitter, that's the question. There's some bemusement at my writing job: one woman is baffled by why you'd bore yourself reading a book never mind writing one, some are enthusiastic, most are supportive and tolerant of my whims; most don't give a damn so long as I do the work.

The cleaners in the arts block have their breaks in a hidden kitchen on the lower ground floor. There are collections for and celebrations to mark significant birthdays and births, First Holy Communions and confirmations of grandchildren in this kitchen. There are retirement breakfasts with egg and onion sandwiches and a glutton's delight of buns and cakes at 8.30 a.m., other retired cleaners coming back in for the occasion. It's the scene of raucous laughter, gossip and vents about ignorant students and staff and occasional tears. One Saturday morning there are cups of tea for us skeleton weekend staff, a shocked sadness over a student who'd killed himself overnight in the toilets, the supervisor tearing after us to stop us going into the aftermath: all thought for the mother getting that horror phone call. It's the security guards who deal with the worst of it.

The ground floor of the arts block is windowless with shabby old brown tiles and bare concrete walls, communist chic. Cleaning here is on a large scale: many public bins to be emptied, large lecture theatres, toilets used by the public. I'm still fairly young with no back problems (yet) and when a grandmotherly cleaner sees me lifting a hoover she grabs it off me and puts it down, saying, Pull don't lift, spare your back. This mantra, Spare your back, stays with me. Take shortcuts and don't be a martyr to the work; as she says, the college will be nowhere to be seen if you end up with chronic back pain.

We enter the lecture rooms in pairs: one takes the far end, one takes the near end, empty the bins first. Then bring a new bin bag around the theatre for the pick-up. We have grabber claws but these are no use for the half-full coffee cups: bend for the cups, place them carefully in the bin bag trying not to burst it with the weight, pick up leftover scarves and hats and headphones and sometimes jewellery, putting them under your oxter for lost property. Some days it feels as if the thirst of whole nations could be quenched by the liquid dregs left in coffee cups on desks and lecture-room floors. The sheer waste is baffling – why pay €4 for a coffee and only drink half?

The most satisfying part is whacking the unfolded tables back down into submission beside the chairs. Then it's hoovering. I've a fantasy of a wireless, plug-less hoover that I could just whizz around with, nipping in and out of tight spots and not having to keep flinging the wire over rows of chairs, stretching it as far as it will go until I have to bend to unplug and re-plug it. Then on to the podium, which I never clean without looking out onto the rows and rows of seats, imagining how lecturers cope with the fear of facing expectant faces every day.

The year before I start work in Trinity, I visit a friend in Hamburg and go see a huge model railway museum called the Miniatur Wunderland. I've always been fascinated by miniatures. From dolls' house furniture to trains and figurines to models of buildings, I love the magical potential of the tiny: their perfection, their scale, their joyful pointlessness. Not quite a child's toy but what the hell use for an adult?

I visit early on a February morning: it's quiet, I'm enthralled. The exhibition is vast: sixteen kilometres of track, more than a thousand trains, many miniature countries, towns and villages. I don't have a smartphone yet, so I take hundreds of photos with my digital camera. I fill pages and pages of a notebook with details of the scenes, my delight growing with each miniature country. What's striking is the detail, the perfect representations of full-sized life: the tiny towel hanging over a balcony to dry, queues for a miniature Portaloo at a festival, tiny diggers doing roadworks, cows being milked, bottles being recycled. There are 200 buttons visitors can push to start trains or fly helicopters or make actual chocolate in the chocolate factory, my very own Willy Wonka moment. This place contains so many of my obsessions – miniatures, magical worlds, trains, it makes me feel so giddy and got. I walk laps, haunting the various lands, filling my notebook with descriptions of scenes that are written so hurriedly and excitedly that the writing is almost illegible, slanting off the page in haste. I may have looked like a corporate spy researching the competition, plotting a covert, copycat miniature land.

I already have the two characters for my next novel, but didn't know where to place them. I almost dance with joy when I realise this is the setting – how could it be anywhere else?

I'm given a training manual and put on a two-day Cleaning Operative Proficiency Course to learn about machines and chemicals. I learn that 'Bathrooms should be cleaned starting at the CLEANEST SECTION FINISHING AT THE DIRTIEST SECTION.' This is the opposite of how I approach my writing, in which I do the biggest, dirtiest job first. I learn how to fold the cloth into four parts, clean a surface with each side and once four surfaces have been cleaned, place the cloth in a bag for washing and start with a clean cloth. This is wonderfully, theoretically hygienic; cleaners don't have that many cloths to work with and few of us have access to washing machines. The assessment requires us to take apart a hoover and reassemble it, as well as to show mastery of the buffer, a machine that incites fear for its temperamental, unpredictable ways. This is harder than any college exam I've done. I furiously scribble notes, trying to remember in what order to take the hoover apart and which bits go where, while the other women on the course look on bemused. Someone remarks I should be used to exams; I explain how three-hour written exams are less stressful than standing up in front of assessors, trying to operate a finicky machine while describing aloud what I'm doing. Also, the pass rate for English exams is 40 per cent; here the pass mark of various tasks is 20 out of 22 or 13 out of 15; small margin for error.

In May, my novel *Eggshells* is launched. I'm trína chéile with excitement and the rawest of nerves. The morning of the launch, I sit in bed with a yellow notebook, trying to write a speech.

The first time I ever gave a presentation was in my second year of speech therapy, the course I originally studied in college before dropping out. Clutching balled-up tissue in my fists, trying to stem the sop of sweat, I shook and rattled and raced through the presentation at such speed I was finished in half the allotted time. Later, when I studied English, I was intimidated by the more vocal students, some of whom were outlandishly wealthy and had attended the same kind of British public schools as the royal family. Although some knew what the minimum wage was, many never worked a summer job – spending their summers 'reading ahead'. They seeped confidence, sprawling almost horizontally with ease. Tutorials unnerved me: I would sit silently confounded, scribbling notes to myself: *Look up DERRIDA, Research SAUSSURE.* Their ease baffled me, their ability to discuss any topic with utter confidence, even if it took me years to realise a lot of what they said was either polysyllabic drivel or taken directly from the introduction.

And the speed of them! No sooner had a lecturer asked a question than one such student began to formulate a response. *How did she think so quickly* I'd wonder as she held forth on any kind of subject. I was slow to gather my thoughts into a coherent argument and would only think of something meaty to say long after I'd left the tutorial (I learnt later that this was known as a *Treppenwitz:* staircase joke in German, coming up with a response on the stairway after the conversation, hindsight).

Notwithstanding the confidence quivers in tutorials, I loved studying English. The two years I had spent studying clinical speech therapy – an intense medical-adjacent course with 9–5 class hours and constant assignments – and the year out of college working to earn some money, helped me to appreciate the pleasure of reading my way through four years of novels, plays and poems, no thoughts to the future: pure bliss. Now that life has gotten busier, I relish the memories of hours-long coffees in Bewley's, afternoons spent shite-talking in pubs, rainy mornings spent reading in bed: what looked like dossing was actually doing coursework.

I didn't get involved in writing for college newspapers or journals; it didn't occur to me then that I could write creatively myself, I was so busy reading other people's creations, but I got my first peek at real writers. I was taught by Brendan Kennelly, Gerald Dawe, Eiléan Ní Chuilleanáin, who I was astonished to learn were renowned poets behind their day job. Until then, writers were at a remove, they existed in a different realm.

Some lecturers took eccentricity to an almost pathological level. The professor who, at the height of foot-and-mouth disease in 2001, brought in a toy sheep and baa-ed his way through the lecture to protest at the UK-government-sanctioned sheep culls. The drama professor who would swoop into tutorials in a black cloak, bellowing ancient Greek and handing out readings in a Greek alphabet that we couldn't understand, casually mentioning the characters' bouts of pederasty. He farted loudly in class one day, which reduced even the most sophisticated student to giggles. Then there was the enthusiastic lecturer who taught Old English and alleviated our terror of exam translation with pretzels and photos of her cats. And the kindness of my first-year tutor who wrote a note at the bottom of an essay to visit her office. She walked me through the essay, line by line, explaining how I could improve my informal style to third-level standards.

Brendan Kennelly's course, The Essay, was a remarkable hour of listening and learning about the world of poets and poetry. In second year, Kennelly awarded me a Composition Prize for an essay I wrote, entitled 'Darkness'. The prize was €12.74, recently converted from £10. It came with the assurance that although the prize was not worth much in monetary terms, the prestige value was incalculable. That was a huge boost to my confidence if not my bank account: my winning essay took the form of a list of things that were dark in colour or theme: possibly the start of my obsession with lists. It strikes me now that I should've taken a notion to continue writing creatively but my head was set on travel: I wanted to go to Japan as soon as I graduated.

After graduating in 2004 I did a TEFL (Teaching English as a Foreign Language) course. My heartrate didn't subside for the entire three weeks of the course. The instructors videoed us practice-teaching so we could review our body language and I grabbed the remote (probably my most confident manoeuvre in the entire course) and fast-forwarded my lesson. I knew I looked hunched and petrified; it would make me even more hunched and petrified to see proof of it, but I took my pass certificate and went to Japan. After initial terrors, I found that teaching children wasn't daunting: they just wanted to be entertained and if you could sneak in a bit of learning, well and good.

When I returned to Ireland I looked for jobs on the basis of not having to give presentations or sit in meetings. The fear was mostly physical: would I fall over, wet myself in abject terror, faint, vomit? The only time I had spoken in public before my book launch was at a reading to mark the end of the creative-writing course I did a few years earlier. To get through that, I drank a double rum and Coke mixed with a couple of pills from a Bolivian 'pharmacy' (a wooden shack near a bus station in La Paz) that the 'pharmacist' convinced me were knock-off Xanax. My legs shook and clattered so much from nerves or dodgy pharmaceuticals that I struggled to stand.

At my launch on a May evening in 2015, the bookshop is hot and crowded, which, combined with nerves, means my back is sweating so much I have to keep staunching the drops against my dress in case a gentle stream of liquid running down my legs is misinterpreted. Where to look? What to say? I decide to just bury my head in the page and read from it. No matter that it's not the most elegant or engaging way to deliver a talk, I can get through it if I focus on pulling out one word at a time. I call it awkward chic and wrap my voice around the first word, then another, and another until it's done. I make it up and down off the platform without falling and that in itself feels like success, never mind the book written. The launch is one of the happiest days of my life. Friends and family have come from Mayo, London, Germany, Australia. It's the week of the marriage equality referendum and some are combining attending my launch with coming home to vote; it's a celebratory week of rainbow bunting and drinking on Capel Street when the result is a resounding yes.

After the release of *Eggshells*, there's a flurry of friends sending pictures of it in various shops. A cleaner friend takes photos of me standing beside a table of my book in Hodges Figgis, I am beaming-proud. There are bunches of flowers and bottles of fizzy wine and cards and cupcakes with my book cover on them and so much good will I'm humbled. I stand outside my local Spar waiting for it to open one Saturday morning to buy *The Irish Times*, tearing at the pages to get to the books section. It's my first review and I'm thrilled. It's an incredible feeling not just to be got, to have my character and intentions understood, but to have the reviewer find things in my book that I hadn't seen myself. There are more mostly decent reviews, the occasional critic complaining there isn't this in it, or it'd be better if there was more of that, or why didn't I write about the other which seems a bit daft in fiction-writing.

After the reviews and interviews, there is a strange kind of anticlimactical limbo, but what it is you're waiting for is unclear. I get some lovely messages and emails and phone calls about my book from people who enjoyed it, and bafflement from others. But what's it really about? is the bewildered question, and, about the main character, What's wrong with her?

My publisher passes on a letter from an Irish woman living in Germany who wrote about her surprise on seeing the name Alphonse Hazard mentioned in *Eggshells*. When I was researching the novel, I walked around Glasnevin Cemetery and found Mr Hazard on a tombstone. I had written in the novel that with a name like that, he could have been a stuntman. This woman writes back to say that he wasn't a stuntman but he was her grandfather. It's a huge moment, like having a message you put in a bottle picked up and read – the feeling that your book can land miles away and still make a connection. And, it shows up my sloppy arithmetic: I thought I'd calculated that any dead person I mentioned would have no living close relatives.

Eggshells gets nominated for a prize and I'm expected to hustle for votes. I send a cringey email to friends and family asking them to please pick me. The awards ceremony is an alternate universe. I manage to find nice, low-key writers to hang out with, but it's a high-octane glamour event that's hard to square with sitting in bed writing. I get an awful attack of the giggles with my sister during a particularly earnest speech; we try to take sneaky photos of each other in front of celebrity authors but the celebrities are onto us. I'm too overawed to approach established writers because I'd either go completely silent or gush incoherently. I eat every bite of the dinner – to the amazement of my agent – and haven't prepared a speech – to the surprise of my publisher – but the results of this prize are fairly predictable: I'm certain I won't have to get up. The next morning, my co-worker shouts the length of the Long Room Library, Well, did you win? No, I say, but I'm grinning with relief that it's over and it takes a while to convince her.

THE KIND OF DIRT YOU HAVE TO CLEAN UP IS dependent on the place you're cleaning. I cleaned in a nursing home and a hospital years ago, which meant conflicting smells of sterility and stew, and a variety of body emissions to wipe up. Context matters: mopping up a puddle of piss in a college is more irritating than its equivalent in a nursing home. An incidence of incontinence is unintentional, and the aim is to clean it up and play it down before it causes distress, but a careless or even deliberate excretion is irritating, it implies the pisser doesn't give a shit. Similarly, I never minded serving even the rudest nursing-home residents meals or dealing with their complaints, whereas I wouldn't have the patience to serve rude customers in a restaurant. Illness and old age can be tough, leeway can be given. I briefly worked in the laundry of a hospital, unthinkingly putting a rubber sheet into the dryer at the hottest setting with a sack of clothes from the men's ward. When I was unable to scrape the burnt rubber off trousers and shirts, I hid the lot in the bottom of a bin and pretended I'd never seen them, feeling bad about leaving a batch of patients trouserless. Cleaning the hospital meant scrubbing in vicious heat in wards and corridors and rooms that were always occupied, unless someone died and a thorough death-scrub was required. I spent a summer cleaning a nursing home in which the residents used to watch TV in silence. Every morning when I walked into the recreation room with the hoover, multiple pairs of feet raised in anticipation; no matter that I hadn't come near them yet: they saw me coming and up went the feet.

I also worked in a private convalescent home in which patients were supposed to get better; they paid too much money to die there. But one woman did manage to die unexpectedly during a post-op convalescence. The matron's main objective was to get the hearse in and out of the grounds without any of the patients noticing and sparking a death-panic. Myself and a carer were dispatched to the sitting room and told to distract the patients. It was a sunny day and we pulled down the blinds, as ordered. This was met with predictable protests from the patients. We said we had a surprise for them and started belting out Christmas carols. It was September. We managed to get a half-hearted chorus going, buoying them on with exuberant conducting while keeping sketch for the hearse to leave with its newly departed cargo. Once the hearse had cleared the window, we abruptly stopped the singing and reopened the blinds, scarpering before any more unanswerable questions could be put to us.

I'm put working with a cleaner in the museum building: she's going for surgery in a few days and I'll cover her work when she's off. As we fill a bucket from a sink in an office facing onto a sunrise over the cricket pitch, she looks out the window and shakes her head saying, Sometimes I think I have the best job in the world.

I too fall in love with this gorgeous building. It's palazzo-style, built in 1857, domed and pillared and grand as anything. An imperial staircase divides into two flights in opposite directions; you can't help but walk down it and feel like a debutante announcing yourself at a royal ball, even if you're sweeping it one step at a time. As extra help, I'm put washing down the marble banisters and Portland stone staircases (which, I find in a Wiki rabbit-hole tunnelling, lines the exterior of Buckingham Palace). I mislay myself in the secret turns and nooks and back stairs and front stairs and side stairs. I walk extra steps not realising I can get from one area to another through a lecture room, instead going all the way downstairs to go back up again. The women working there are friendly and welcoming and I find myself wishing for an area like this. Away from the gaze of the supervisor in the arts block, this building makes its own rules.

My favourite task is: scrubbing a tea-stained kitchen sink with cream cleaner and a yellow sponge, badgering the steel up to a decent shine.

I start researching security-guard work for my second novel. I try to imagine myself back to the Miniatur Wunderland by looking at videos and photos on the website and on various fan pages: where there are model trains there are obsessive fans. I go through my own photos and notebooks. I read my scrawled details of scenes, mundane or fantastical or surreally random: miniature people practising CPR on a miniature dummy, a miniature alien watching a play in an amphitheatre, miniature people riding a dragon, a miniature clown in a garden centre under a wedding in a hotel, a miniature horse sitting casually in a convertible, a kangaroo on a bicycle in a miniature Tour de France, a car being winched up from the bottom of a lake, a fire in miniature Hamburg. There are countless pints of beer being drunk, blow jobs being given and a recurring theme of monks perving on women unseen.

I need to place my character R (he hasn't been named yet), in various locations in the Wunderland and for him to interact with the exhibits. But a security guard's job is watching. And I don't remember seeing any roving security guards moving around the exhibition. I change R. to be a cleaner. This gives him more agency, he'll have an excuse to interact with the exhibit when he's cleaning it, and as he'll be working hours before visitors come, he'll have access to the empty museum. And because I work as a cleaner, no research is needed.

Things that annoy me most about my cleaning job:

> Popcorn.
> Ignorance.
> Butty little screws that jut out of mirrors snagging my cloth.
> New, unwashed cloths that leave a lint trail.
> Toilets left in a condition that stop just short of a dirty protest.
> Equipment that doesn't work. When I first started, I told my supervisor that my hoover wasn't working and asked for a new one, causing a bout of hysterical laughter between her and the house-man. The house-man led me to a tiny room full of hoover parts – a makeshift hoover hospital – told me to take what I needed, and handed me a roll of black tape to cobble it together.

When I give a talk at my first literary festival to promote *Eggshells* in early 2016, I discuss various aspects of writing and don't mention my cleaning job. Afterwards, I'm asked by an audience member if I write full-time and I say no, my day job is a cleaner. From then on, the questions are almost all about my cleaning job. I now realise how strange a life choice it seems for some people.

I'm nominated for another prize, which again I know will not come my way, but I have more nerves this time because all the nominees have to go up on stage for a photo. I don't participate in raffles for that reason. (A like-minded friend once chewed and swallowed the raffle tickets we'd gotten at a work Christmas party so she wouldn't have to walk up to collect her prize.) Yet again I arrange my face in the loser grin; at least I've had practice.

I feel a surge of excitement being at this festival. Staying in a hotel room on my own, making a glutton of myself at the buffet breakfast with no co-breakfaster to blame for the pile of empty plates, being surrounded by people who write for a living, including names I'd heard of and thought were so far removed from my life. It's exhilarating, a glimpse at what being a writer, as opposed to writing a book, might be.

A kindly couple from the festival offer me a lift back to Dublin and I gratefully accept; it'll be quicker than the bus. I sit in the back seat with another writer who'll be dropped to the train station. Shortly after she gets out, I'm chatting with the couple when my screen lights up with the other writer's name. I open the message thinking she's left something in the car but no, she has written one question: *Do you know who you're in the car with?* I feel a chill, imagining a Fred and Rose West situation, but surely she would have warned me if they were known serial killers, or killers at least. No, I reply, who are they? Bill and Denise Whelan is the answer. I've been chatting away with Mr

Riverdance about Limerick and writing (*Do write your life story, it's a lovely thing to hand down to your kids even if it's never published*) without having a notion who he is. I come clean, mortified, change tack to: *When* your memoir is published …

Things I've learnt from cleaning:

1. Your dossing room (your 'office') will be the cleanest room in your area because whenever you hear footsteps you have to leap up and let on you're cleaning. (A cleaner's office could be the actual office of a lecturer who is on sabbatical or who doesn't come into work early, or it could be a hidden nook or corner of a library that you can take an unofficial break in.) A supervisor once happened on me sitting in an office, frantically typing on my laptop, trying to meet a pressing writing deadline during a quiet moment. I just had time to close the laptop and hop up with my cloth (top tip: always keep a cloth and spray handy). Maybe it was my guilty face, but she decided to inspect the room, running her fingers over the bookshelves (dust-free), peered closely at the table (spotless), checked the floors (crumb-free). My heart was thudding when she approached the laptop: if she felt its warmth, I couldn't pass it off as the lecturer's whose room it was. My supervisor left, congratulating me on such a clean office. I never used the laptop in work again.

2. The popularity of a building is inversely proportional to the difficulty cleaning it. Old buildings have no lifts and years of ingrained dirt, but are most visited and on every tourist's to-see list. I've heard laments about the tragedy of historic old benches being taken out of the museum building and replaced by modern seats, but cleaners don't lament the loss.
3. Wet the mop more than you think, the going will be easier.
4. Never wash the cups in the kitchens: the staff will come to expect it and treat you like a skivvy. This can turn into an intense game of chicken. A shared office I clean has daily cups and plates and cutlery left in the sink, stains accumulating around them, offending me. I itch to wash them and get the cream cleaner into the sink to scour it but I force myself to leave them, like trying not to give in to a toddler's demands even though it's easier in the short term. I clean the sink around the growing pile of cutlery and cups, surely the definition of passive aggressive housekeeping. Eventually when the office staff run out of crockery and succumb to washing up, I rush in to fully clean the sink.
5. Damp dusting is more efficient than dry dusting.
6. It's better to stay busiest when you haven't slept. If you stop or slow down, you'll flag. Do your toughest jobs (polishing brasses, digging at the knottiest carpets with a hoover, scraping chewing gum from the underside of desks) when tiredest.

7. Always carry a prop (cloth and cleaning spray, dustpan and brush, bin bag) if you're going to another cleaner's area for a chat.
8. The soap dispensers in the gents' toilets seldom run low.
9. When alcohol is involved, a cardboard recycle bin can seem like a legitimate toilet.
10. Never clear up what looks like rubbish from the contemporary art gallery on campus. When I briefly cleaned the Douglas Hyde Gallery, a cleaner told me how he had previously swept up and binned empty Tayto wrappers and Coke cans from the floor of the exhibition space, only to be told afterwards that it was an art installation he'd just demolished. Check with your supervisor before you touch anything, he warned me. Ask her: is this art or is it rubbish because I haven't a fucking breeze.

I'm put dusting books and shelves in the Lecky Library, then cleaning chewing gum from the undersides of the tables. If you're a person who's never stuck their used gum under a table, it's hard to imagine why anyone would do it. Something about the muffled carpeting of the Lecky is very soothing. I deep-clean the desk surfaces, grey-blue Formica with indents of rivers and tributaries, the better to catch the dirt. At the bottom of the stairs on the lower ground floor is the desk that I favoured as a student. I remember laying out pages and pages of notes and hand-writing essays about twentieth-century female novelists, never suspecting that I'd be a 21st-century female novelist. I'm put deep-cleaning tall library stacks in the basement on my own, shelves and shelves of books and journals, which could be a decent setting for the chase scene of an action movie. I can picture hiding between the shelves then overturning them to thwart the baddie.

One morning I'm hoovering the exam hall, a beautiful, echoey, eighteenth-century building with a vaulted ceiling. It's dark first thing but fills magically with sunlight when dawn comes in, dust-motes landing on the chandelier that's someone else's job to dust. One of my favourite things in this job is being alone in gorgeous old rooms at sunrise. I hoover the chessboard floor tiles, obeying sudden urges to leap from black to white in a one-woman fixed-to-win game – I'm Alice in *Through the Looking Glass*, I'm Ron during the high-stakes chess game in *Harry Potter*. It's nice to have freedom of movement in this room, having sat and sweated my way through exams here, struggling to fill the notebooks allotted, agog at students doing the same exam asking for extra paper.

The summer following my final exams, I was covering for the cleaner who usually cleaned the English department on the fourth floor of the arts block in Trinity. I cleaned an office with boxes that contained an exam script I had written the previous month. It was like another life in that box, layers of life, differently lived, at full-tilt collision. It felt strange, as if the English student version of myself had been boxed up and the worker version, soon-to-be-traveller version, had taken over. I wasn't too bothered by my results. I never did very well in English exams, compared to essays when I had more time to gather my thoughts, so my expectations were moderate. My graduation was held in this exam hall more than a decade ago, in Latin that was Dutch to me. I remember trying to shush my mother's grievances about Trinity's grabby colonial past: 'Why does Trinity have the Book of Kells, isn't it about time they gave it back?' I don't believe in ghosts but this room surely holds such extremes of emotion, fear and elation; there must be some particles of it in the air somewhere.

For each new area I clean, there's a different bunch of keys, the easiest ones with master keys to open all the offices, some with different keys I need to learn for each room. When the cleaner who's going on holidays or under the knife shows me around (or their co-worker if they're out on surprise sick) I write door codes in my notebook, a blue-smocked dinosaur with pencil and paper when other spares use their phone Notes app.

My least favourite place to clean is the GMB, the Graduates Memorial Building, which hosts the debating society's events, even though I love the building. It is a neo-Gothic Victorian building and I love the spookiness of the dark chambers, the windy staircase, the huge stained-glass window. The morning after a debate, the function rooms are in a depressingly squalid condition that reminds me of the 'gentlemen's' club in the

Jeeves and Wooster books, in which upper-class buffoons had food fights to amuse themselves and to hell with the cleaners. I'm warned by the cleaner showing me around to take it handy unlocking doors, that occasionally there's a straggling debater in a crumpled tuxedo asleep on the floor of a council room. She says I'll know from the bang of drink if they're dead or just dead drunk. The attitude of these students towards cleaners intrigues me, or rather, the absence of attitude: the best that could be said is that it doesn't occur to them when they're lobbing popcorn across rooms or throwing drink around that somebody will have to clean it up.

We bring the dirty delph to the sink for them to wash themselves. I think of the sign that editor Mary-Kay Wilmers taped above the tea station in the *London Review of Books*' offices: 'Please wash your cup. There's nobody who doesn't resent doing other people's washing up.' (I love the wording. I can't explain why it is that washing someone's cup feels so skivvy-ish when cleaning a toilet doesn't.)

In my fortnight-stint cleaning the GMB, I leave a glass of milk well enough alone on a table on my first morning. Over the next two weeks, in a warm room, the milk changes consistency to a clotty mess of foul-smelling sludge, but still neither the milk-drinker nor their friends wash the glass. I occasionally think of the Great Dairy Stand-Off and imagine that the combination of ignorance, tenacity and sense of entitlement that enabled these debaters to ignore the clabbered milk will facilitate them to go on to great things.

I'm tasked with cleaning the Old Library and Book of Kells. To get there, I enter the arts block, go down the stairs past the supervisor's office, through the usually alarmed fire exit door into the lower ground floor of the Lecky Library, walk the red carpet through the Lecky, up the few steps into the Berkeley foyer, take a sharp turn left, down a half-flight of steps into the study space, through an innocuous-looking fire door, up the steps, walk along the tunnels where buckets catch raindrops from leaks, go around the corner, call the ancient clanky lift and get jolted out at the Long Room, the main chamber of the Old Library. Or I knock on the locked door of the gift shop and wait for the cleaner to notice me over the sound of her hoover and let me in.

The Long Room is, as the name suggests, fairly long. It was built in the early 1700s, with the barrel-vaulted ceiling and more bookcases added in 1860 when the original shelves were full. The shelves were full because since 1801 Trinity had been 'given the right' to claim a free copy of every book published in Britain and Ireland. I'm torn between pride that my book will be claimed by Trinity and bafflement by how a wealthy institution wouldn't pay for the books.

I love being here on my own, surrounded by hundreds of thousands of musty old books and marble busts of dead, thinky men. A bulb is on the fritz in one of the alcoves, it fizzes and flashes, adding to the atmosphere.

I buff the brown lino of the floor that runs the length of the Long Room Library, those 65 metres putting the long into the Long Room – almost the length of an indoor running track. Every buffer machine is different, like temperamental, elderly relatives with their own peculiar habits and notions that you have to adapt to.

The cleaner I'm covering for has me trained in on the figaries of this particular buffer: where to rest the machine (low on your hips) how gently to manoeuvre it side to side, how to go with it rather than force it (like a lot of cleaning tips, a metaphor for life maybe). I'm fairly confident but confidence is of no use the first day I buff alone. I walk the length of the floor buffing gently from side to side, then turn slowly to buff the next strip of lino, like a groundsman mowing a football pitch. On one of my turns, I twist the machine too quickly and it takes umbrage, skiting off in its preferred direction, knocking me off my feet before scudding across the floor and bashing into a glass case containing a folio of a precious manuscript. I'm dazed on the floor, crawling frantically across the lino, wondering how much damage is done, if I'll have to pay for it. Fortunately, the machine is shaped like a capital L: the bumper part of the buffer has crashed into the metal bottom of the case, the glass display is intact. I coax it back into obedience like a contrary pet and we sway gently together over the next couple of weeks, getting up the most satisfying shine on the brown lino: easily provable if I haven't the work done.

Part of my job in this area is dusting the leather-bound books with a feather duster at 9 a.m. as the first coachloads of

American tourists arrive. They take pictures, shouting, Look, the janitor! while I duck and dive from the action shot, the wild beast going about her business in her natural habitat.

I cover the work of cleaning the gift shop on the ground floor, which sells Trinity trinkets and tat, including my novel. Being left alone in a shop makes me nervous I'll be blamed if an item goes missing, or I'll crash into a display with the arm of my hoover and break something, or many things. But when I'm alone in the little room next to the gift shop, polishing the glass of the Book of Kells, it's bliss. I also love polishing the display case containing pigments used to make ink, thinking back to my obsession with the pigments on display in the Chester Beatty that made their way into my first novel. The alchemy of a pinch of beautifully coloured powder that can be transformed into finely wrought letters on a manuscript page.

I clean the Manuscripts department on the second floor, spraying and wiping the desks of the Early Printed Books department with their foam bookstands for precious old texts, remembering being brought here as a student to see an early edition of Shakespeare. I'm cleaning here one early January morning, just after the Christmas holidays, nine months into the job. It's bitterly cold, the rooms haven't been heated over the Christmas, cleaning hard and fast will only get me so warm. I layer my coat on my lap in a little hidden corner and drink from a flask of coffee I've brought, to warm me up. I go downstairs to the Long Room Library in the clanky old lift at 9 a.m. to do my last thirty minutes of dry-dusting a section of the books (the dusting is divided alphabetically among four cleaners). When I emerge from the lift, a boss, a stickler for rules, walks over. I wince – a cleaner on a 3.5-hour day has no business smelling of coffee. The boss-lady asks an open-ended question about my Christmas. I keep it brief. She leans closer and asks how my writing is going, I keep it even briefer, giving up on sentences and resorting to monosyllables with my mouth mostly closed while she pointedly sniffs the air around my mouth. I'm trying to talk through the grittiest of teeth, swatting the question back to her about her own Christmas, but she's having none of it. Eventually, after getting me to agree that the 3.5-hour cleaners aren't entitled to a break, she asks if I'd like my own area. It's the top floor of the arts block, a modern area, brighter and airier than the older floors beneath, built onto the arts block when I was a student. I say yes please and I start immediately.

When the sixth floor was newly built, I used to go up with friends to eat lunch looking out over Nassau Street, being caught by security and reprimanded for eating in front of the No Eating signs. Now I'm the one cleaning, I hope the no-eating rule is obeyed. The surfaces are still new enough to be fairly easy to clean, the academic staff are friendly, the sunrises from the floor-to-ceiling windows are magnificent.

I time my hoovering around the sunrise in an east-facing office that catches the light beautifully, marking spring with an earlier sunrise every week.

I love it up here – my own area! – but it's busy. I clean two-thirds of the sixth floor; another woman comes in at 7 a.m. to clean the other third. My roster tells me the conference room + event space is to be hoovered and properly cleaned once a week; I do it at least three times a week. No roster contains time slots for the after-effects of boozy conferences: mopping floors pocked with wine spills and trampled canapés, hacking the hoover at pastry crumbs dug into carpets, lugging bags and bags of wine bottles, trays and trays of stale sandwiches to the outdoor bins. If I complain to my supervisor, I'm told they've promised to clean up after themselves, promises as empty as those of errant children saying they'll tidy away their toys. I also clean two kitchens, a small library, many individual offices and an enormous open-plan office, two flights of stairs, men's toilets, women's toilets, a disabled toilet and a long corridor.

I parcel out my day into half-hour chunks. On busy post-conference mornings I race to fit the last half-hour's overhanging work into the current half-hour's. I usually start with the toilets, get them done before people start coming in. One morning, during a week of back-to-back conferences, the conference organiser approaches to sweet-talk me into cleaning up after last night's conference before this morning's one. Even though I empathise with the pressure she's under, the gap between expectation and possibility is glaring: I have a large area outside of this conference room to clean, there will be complaints if I don't. Nobody – except the cleaner I share the floor with who comes to my aid after particularly messy conferences – understands just how much work is involved. Nobody will defend our realities because they don't see the first-thing filth, or even if they do, they just want it done. Nobody, not even your supervisor, knows how much or how little you do; the night elves secretly, thanklessly making shoes. (I've come to hate the word 'just': if you could *just*, could you *just*. Usually uttered by those who are *just* too busy themselves to do the task that is *just* not in my job description.)

I am a cleaner. Some people are uncomfortable with the word 'cleaner'. I've been called 'the person who cleans'. I appreciate the delicate effort to not offend but it's the long way around to say the same thing, and the word cleaner is nothing to be ashamed of. I've been called a maid or a janitor. A janitor has more of a cleaning + maintenance caretaking role, which makes me more of an American maid, but maid smacks of servant, which has the bang of servitude off it. I clean up after people to a point: that point being emptying bins, not washing up or tidying up after people. (I work in housekeeping but I'm nobody's housekeeper.) Cleaning lady is used by well-meaning people, to take the edge off the bare cleaner. I like the lady part, it's so old-fashioned, particularly when we have a growing number of male cleaners in the college. In *A Manual for Cleaning Women*, Lucia Berlin writes: 'I never think of myself as a cleaning lady, although that's what they call you, their lady or their girl.' In Trinity Housekeeping, we call ourselves 'the women'.

Synonyms for cleaners: skivvy, servant, charwoman, slavey, bedder, The Help, scrubber: which can be used for prostitute too, an ambiguity I thought of when I was unemployed and job-hunting for short-term work on Gumtree. I typed cleaner into the search box and requests popped up for cleaners to wear French maids' uniforms (provided) and be comfortable with the (male) homeowners lying on the sofa watching while the applicant cleaned the apartment in uniform ('Must be able to work in heels').

Rolling toilet cleaning is the most thankless job. Trying to get into a cubicle around a queue of pissers and shitters who are irritated by your presence yet presumably expect toilets that are magically, constantly spotless.

I NEVER DREAMED OF BEING A WRITER AS A CHILD, I just loved reading. I played with words the way other kids play with toys, spending long car journeys from Dublin to Mayo rearranging letters in names on shopfronts. With some friends in primary school I invented a sign language and wrote the directions in a notebook, but I took it to extremes, constantly inventing new signs for different words, and was disappointed by the fleetingness of my pals' interest. I wrote stories in white Homestead copybooks, outside of homework, for fun. I loved playing post office or librarian with a real ink stamper and imagined myself a postmistress or librarian; my childhood fantasies never featured princesses or weddings. My parents knew the postmistress in the post office in my father's hometown of Belmullet, which was also a sweet- and toy shop, and I thought this might just be the best job in the world.

I used my parents' old green Olivetti typewriter to belt out pieces of written text. Not so much joined-up stories as clues for treasure hunts, riddles, notes, silly rhymes. The magic of clacking buttons and seeing your thoughts appear on paper. As a teenager, I wrote letters to friends during the school holidays, testing the postal system by sending chopped-up pieces of cereal boxes with stamps on. When letters to my own friends weren't enough, I signed up for a pen pal service, which matched me with pen pals in various countries until the joy I felt at receiving a letter was soon outweighed by the guilt I felt at the time it took me to reply. My siblings and I wrote messages in bottles and flung them off Mayo cliffs on our summer holidays. One letter found its way to the north of England and we ended up with a letter from a girl our age who became a pen pal. The magic of being responded to – it felt like the opening of a Famous Five book.

During summer holidays in Mayo and Connemara I read in the car, in my uncle's van, in the hayshed, stalks of hay scratching my bare legs. I read the contents of Belmullet library dry: I read Famous Five, Secret Seven, Adventurous Four, Nancy Drew, The Three Investigators and Hardy Boys mysteries. I read mysteries and secrets into the bogs and cliffs and deserted coves near my uncle's house, I still can't walk there without imposing on the landscape my childhood images of treasure maps and secret letters and smugglers in sea-caves. I read old copies of *Reader's Digest* in my granny's house, marvelling at the near misses of ordinary people caught in disaster and mayhem. I moved onto terrible romance novels in my teenage years, stalling at the teen shelf of the library.

Around that time, I ran cross-country in school, then I finished my first marathon aged seventeen and got hooked on distance running. My hearing has been poor since childhood; perhaps I've been drawn to solitary pursuits like reading and running because they allowed me to relax in my own world and not have to listen out for external cues. School could be tiring, having to tune out background noise and strain for the teacher's voice; running and reading gave me restful autonomy. I ran a few more marathons in my twenties before entering Comrades, an ultramarathon in South Africa, in 2010. To qualify for this 55-mile ultra, I needed to run a marathon in under five hours. I entered the Dublin Marathon, broke a toe and couldn't run. So I did the Valencia Marathon with my brother a few months later. A mile before the end, I felt something give in my knee. I kept running in a dazzle of pain, seemingly unable to stop until the finish clock at 3:59:59. When I got back to Ireland, an MRI showed a tear in the meniscus. Around the time I should have been running Comrades, I was undergoing knee surgery, which failed to fully fix the problem, and physio could only do so much. I gave up on the ultramarathon dream and settled for an evening class in creative writing, bashing out my first unpublishable short stories and essays before starting to write my first novel after the course finished. I sometimes wonder if I had to choose, whether I'd run or write; my answer varies depending on the day.

I'm cleaning the men's toilets one morning at 6 a.m. This floor can only be accessed with a swipe card. I'm alone up here until my co-worker starts in an hour. As I'm scrubbing one of the urinals, I notice someone lifting the sweeping brush I've jammed slantways in the doorway to keep it open. The door swings shut and a man walks towards me. He smells of alcohol and is smiling. I start to say, The toilets are closed for cleaning, but as I'm talking, he stands at the urinal beside me, unzips and starts pissing, grinning all the while. I'm torn between anger and fear; it's not ideal to be stood beside an arrogant asshole with his prick in his hand when there's nobody else around. I leave the toilets and wait in my cubby for him to finish, fuming, my mind whirring with what I could shout at him, what chemical I could spray at his exposed bits, who I could tell. I settle for the usual ranting to my co-worker when she comes in. Nothing will probably be done if I complain further (when you gotta go you gotta go, don't be so uptight!) and making enemies of the people you clean up after is not advisable.

The walk to work takes thirty minutes from my front door to the front gate of Trinity College. For most of the year it's dark. I pass a primary school where a man wearing a headlamp unloads crates of milk from a van. When I reach Phibsboro crossroads, there are more people around walking quickly, arms swinging, head down, power on. Normal traffic rules do not apply at 5.30 a.m.: cars and vans go fast, bikes use footpaths, traffic lights are more suggestion than direction. At the crossroads one dark rainy morning, a driver looks to the right and starts driving on red, he doesn't see me coming from the left. The bumper nudges me off my feet and onto the bonnet, the driver is aghast and apologetic. I wear hi-vis from now on and never take a green man for granted.

Drivers of taxis, buses and lorries gather outside the 24-hour Centra, drinking coffee – I imagine them sorting out the world before it gets going for the day. I pass a prison and a hospital and no matter how tired I am, nothing makes me feel more grateful to be out and about under my own steam than those buildings. Buses head for their routes; at this hour you'd be forgiven for thinking Entering Service was a popular city destination.

My mouth waters as I pass the café where a man bakes bread in the kitchen at the back. The early part of the week is the quietest, bar the odd request for money. Most drunks at this hour are focused hard on moving one foot in front of the other, trudging as if through syrup on the epic journey homeward, or slowly manoeuvring chips into mouths. The occasional carouser wants to chat but a shouted, I'm going to work! breaks the spell. People are sleeping or just waking up in sleeping bags and tents, more and more tents over the years I walk to work.

One morning a joyridden car veers wildly across the road and onto the footpath before lurching around a corner. I call the guards before realising I can't describe a car that was going too fast for me to see the make, the reg, the type: saloon? Hatchback? I don't know, I tell the 999 operator, it's straight down at the back not sticky-out like the ones we used to draw in school.

If I'm making good time on O'Connell Street, clean laundry bags are being dropped off at hotels and hairdressers; if I'm running late, the dirty laundry bags are being taken away. Bread is being delivered to hotels and guesthouses; a newsagent unlocks a metal box outside his shop and pulls out a bale of newspapers. There's occasionally the makings of a fight outside the fast fooderies on O'Connell Street, or an actual fight, which seems bizarre while you're sober. On this street, I experience several incidents of young lads coming on strong for cash: this is no addiction desperation, these are calculated attempts on someone they presume is drunk and vulnerable. Again, a loud, I'm going to work! shows sobriety and an ability to hold onto my bag and sometimes diffuses a situation. I also wear a €12 Casio wristwatch for occasions when I'm asked the time. One morning, two lads with an electric scooter are being quite insistent that they need to see the time on my phone as opposed to my watch when they spy a man staggering out of Sackville Place fixing his zipper. He's quickly relieved of his phone and wallet before he even realises he has been had.

As I pass a certain street lamp on a quiet road near the Mater Hospital, it flickers off. When I reach College Green, a light on the roof of the bank flickers – maybe Dumbledore is following me around. The front of Trinity is often lit up a certain colour: I puzzle over it trying to match it to an event or cause, tell myself to google it later and forget till the next morning's same thought at the same place. I say good morning to the security guard (hoping the grouch isn't on today), clock in, ask for my bunch of keys. Security are finishing as we are starting, we operate at opposite sides of the shift. The walkers and cyclists arrive in straggles, passengers in clumps: the Ballymun bus (whose driver sometimes drops them at the door, an unofficial taxi service), the Finglas bus, the Tallaght Luas. There's a ghost bus that appears on no timetables or bus-stop screens but which appears and brings women into work. (Ghost buses are usually a negative phenomenon, expected buses that don't turn up: this is more like the *Harry Potter* one, an unofficial, much-wanted extra.) I walk through Front Square, lit by old-fashioned, dim lamps that remind me of Narnia. One of the lights in the Long Room Library flickers, the lights in the rest of the building flicker on in ordered rows like dominoes, or patchwork on randomly. Foxes skulk about the huge dumpsters; seagulls glow white against the lights from cranes, jawing over scraps of food. From mid-April there's bright in the sky when I arrive into the college; I don't feel so at odds with the world.

When I sweep one-cent and two-cent coins into a dustpan and am too lazy to take them out, I think of The KLF burning a million pounds in the 1990s, and wonder if what I'm doing is illegal, destroying legal tender.

When you start work, all keen and gullible, you're susceptible to being played and having work offloaded onto you. As a student-cleaner I was green but I'm cannier now if older hens play the poor mouth to trick younger chicks into doing their work. When it was suggested by a workshy cleaner that a young person would do a better job cleaning her stairs, I explained I was struggling enough with my own stairs with my gammy post-op knee. Some cleaners do this job because they're not built for daytime work with people. One woman who previously worked in retail was told after a particularly heated encounter with a customer (in which she congratulated herself on not reefing the customer across the counter and battering her) that she might be better suited to a job that didn't involve dealing with people.

One morning after I clock off, I go to a café near Trinity to write. The lad at the till spies the Trinity ID card in my wallet and tells me that Trinity staff and students get a discount with their ID. That's great, I say, handing him my card. I'm studying in Trinity, he says. Ah, I say, what course? English. That's what I studied too, I say. Oh? He says brightly, are you lecturing there now? No, I say, I'm cleaning there now. To say his face fell sounds metaphorical but it was literal.

I've thought more about my choice of work since I was asked by audience members about cleaning in the book festival in Limerick in 2016 because it's usually one of the first things to come up during interviews or literary events. It was a deliberate decision to take an early-morning, physical job that would work well with writing. I've always been drawn to manual work for its sense of completion and satisfaction. I spent childhood summers on my uncle's small farm in west Mayo and loved helping to wash out the milk churns after the cows were milked, clean the milking parlour and the animal bedding afterwards. It's a strange teenager who will willingly get up early on school holidays to shovel cow dung, but I found a quiet joy in the ritual of it. As a student, I earned money by delivering post at Christmas, caring for elderly people in nursing homes and in their own homes, child-minding and cleaning in hospitals and nursing homes. I prefer: routine work that is predictable and constant. If I was wealthy, I'd hire someone to cook for me but would be happy to clean my own toilet: cooking is the drudge-work for me. A meal worked on for hours is eaten in minutes; a bathroom stays cleaner for longer.

I like having a job completely unrelated to writing and the feeling of having done the physical work before sitting down to write. When I was training for marathons, I used to do my long runs on a Saturday and come home to an almighty feed on the sofa in front of a James Bond film or a Miss Marple mystery. I also like having co-workers, people to discuss the weather with, the darkness of the mornings, the public transport failings, the price of bread. There's weekly chat about the special offers and deals in the German discount supermarkets, which bargains are worth it. When slabs of Coke or Fanta are heavily discounted or tins of biscuits or tubs of sweets are half-price at Christmas, one of the cleaners who drives or has access to a car will offer to pick up some for those of us who don't drive. I know things about my co-workers that I don't know about my close friends – what time of day they shower at, what they ate for dinner last night, what they wear in bed.

Cleaners mostly shower at night.

COMPARED TO WRITING, CLEANING IS BOUND BY limits of space and time. I work 3.5 hours every morning. My hours must add up to 17.5 hours a week. I like the simple process of addition and subtraction, no space for doubt or ambiguity. Precise half-hours are mapped out in my work rota: I must have this lecture room cleaned by this time in order to get to that lecture room before students start coming in. My job is counted in rooms and square metres, hours and minutes. I've heard menial jobs referred to, often disparagingly, as 'leave-your-brain-at-the-door' jobs, but I'd see it as mindful in its mindlessness. There is, almost oxymoronically, a freedom in the structure of cleaning, the nature of being constricted to certain spaces within certain times frees my mind to work away. I often find myself in total immersion in the rhythm of buffing or hoovering or scrubbing, which seems to spur unconnected thoughts and allows my brain to wander to my characters or to a plot problem.

The causality also appeals to me. A room is dirty. I clean it. Trinity pays me for that hour. My job is directly transactional. I clock in at 5.50 a.m. and clock out at 9.20 a.m. Cleaners talk in minutes and hours: you put in your hours, you do your hours and go, what are your hours? You give your supervisor ten minutes because you took ten minutes yesterday. Don't be going over your hours: going over your hours is putting in unpaid minutes and is seen as the height of idiocy. Some of my co-workers are horrified by retired professors who keep coming back into the college to research and teach the odd lecture – they pity these 'poor eejits'. Work stops at sixty-five, unless you need to carry on for the cash. You've put in your years, you've earned your rest.

Successful people usually emphasise the variety of their jobs and how no day is the same. That would be nightmarish to me: I crave the ease of sameness. An admin job would be my own personal hellscape for its lack of completion, multitasking requirements, the need to react to constant requests, and meetings. I'm utterly baffled by the meetings and conferences that office workers describe, I can't see them as anything but complete wastes of time. There's no politics in my job: no spoofing, no waffling, no pretending to know things you haven't a clue about. There's no ladder to climb: you're a cleaner, or you go for promotion to supervisor, which few cleaners want to do: supervisor positions are difficult to fill and usually require external applicants. You do your work – it's obvious whether you've done it or not – you get paid.

Cleaners' communication with supervisors is carried out through phone calls or actual visits to your work area. Your supervisor phones or visits your area for a chat, the issue is sorted in minutes. Because the building is empty in the early morning but for cleaners, we find each other by roaring, names echoing through the building, *Caroliiiiiiiiine!*

With no meeting agendas, no exchange of work emails, we sometimes know one another's first names only. My brother asks if I know a woman who cleans his friend's house and works in Trinity. He knows only the surname, I know only first names unless I see my co-workers' wage slips. I have to ask my supervisor for the surname of a cleaner for a sympathy card when her mother dies, even though we've been friends for years.

Having to show up for my cleaning job means I tend to prioritise it over my writing. I can't decide I'm not feeling inspired to clean that day. Writing is unquantifiable, immeasurable, it's never done. Writing can be horribly subjective. The objectivity of a room that is clean or dirty appeals to me in contrast. When asked, I say that I'm a writer and cleaner: cleaning pays the bills while writing is sporadic income. Because I'm not commercially viable, it's hard to view writing as a career. (My advance for one novel was less than two weeks' part-time cleaning wages; that is to say, 3.5 hours of cleaning work paid more than three years of writing.)

I enjoyed the sociability of cleaning a hospital and nursing home in my twenties but it involved shift work and weekend work. Cleaning a university is better suited to my current life. My work is done before staff and students arrive, so it's quiet, contemplative, solitary yet a little bit social because I have co-workers – cleaners, security guards and maintenance staff. I work Monday to Friday and one Saturday in five, the same shift every morning. I like the rhythm of the academic year, the clumps of busy teaching weeks with calm reading weeks in between, when you can catch up on the bigger jobs, the deep-cleans when students finish their summer exams and before conferences and summer schools begin.

When I was optimistically setting up this life, I had vaguely ascetic notions, inspired by Haruki Murakami and the monastic early-to-rise lifestyle he described in *What I Talk About When I Talk About Running*. I imagined myself getting up early to clean, straight to the desk after work to write, doing some exercise and eating healthily, then early to bed. But I hadn't factored in that I'm not a morning person: I have to fight my body clock to get myself out of bed; I forgot that I love junk food and staying up late watching terrible romcoms on Netflix. Even at my peak marathon fitness, I never let training come between me and my junk-food intent (the extra running gave me extra chocolate leeway).

I take to writing in cafés on mornings I'm particularly tired, mainlining caffeine and sugar. I get to know the quiet ones where I can squirrel myself away in a corner. This gets me a couple of hours, work under my belt, I go home to nap, then wake up and write from the bed. Gert, my female character, is coming through easy. I hadn't thought much about her life, I had been more focused on her brother's backstory, but now her experiences and preoccupations are making themselves felt. She's beginning to overtake her brother as a person of interest; I have to work to keep both characters going, give them equal time, and keep them in different voices.

Working so early means my evening social life is more restricted. I take to meeting friends for breakfast: either other cleaners or friends on shift work or sporadically employed. Breakfast is the one meal in which you can order sweet treats as a main course and not be considered daft. I sometimes meet fellow buffet breakfast fiends for hotel breakfasts, trying to outdo each other on voracious buffet runs, empty plates piled high between us. Or, if I have a thirst on me, the occasional session with a willing friend in a dark and cosy early house on Capel Street where 9.30 a.m. feels like 5 p.m.

I take part in several book festivals around Ireland the summer of 2016 to talk about *Eggshells*. It feels exhilarating to meet other writers and talk shop, to have a different set of co-workers to talk about my different job with. I've run out of holidays in my cleaning job and have to beg for some unpaid leave to manage the festivals – this is my first inkling that the job I take to facilitate my writing is also hindering it.

I attend a literary festival in the south-west during a heatwave. I've taken two buses from Dublin (I can't drive, it veers between a phobia and a to-do list item on my braver days) and am in a lather of sweat by the time I get to the hotel. I check in, race up to the bedroom and have the speediest of showers, then go downstairs to meet the other writer on my panel, William Wall, in the lobby. William is relaxed and friendly, a seasoned writer in several genres. After a few minutes, chit-chat, he asks if I have my talk prepared. I giggle nervously. What talk? The 25-minute talk on Writing the Short Story we were asked to give, he says. He takes a brochure from a nearby table, opens it onto our event, and there it is: a photo of me and William beside the title of the event, Writing the Short Story. I stare at my face, wondering who this person is. Could she have written a short story? I start to sweat again, my shower forgotten. But I've never published a short story, I say, I've only written a novel. William laughs. No seriously, I've tried but I've never had a short story published.

The moderator arrives and greets us. I explain I'm in a spot of bother. He shakes his head and asks, Where did they get you from? I'm standing at the door of the hotel. I can see the bus stop from there and I get the fiercest of urges to run, run, *run*, just flee, leave my stuff behind and head for the hills. I don't flee.

I explain there must have been a misunderstanding, I can't talk to a room full of people looking for tips on improving their short-story writing. I'd be a colossal fraud. In an enormous act of decency, William suggests he scrap his talk and we have a general conversation about writing, novels and short stories. I'm overwhelmingly grateful, after all the work he put into his side of things, but I watch the attendees arriving into the function room in droves feeling sick.

I sweat through the event, feeling bad for people who paid to sit and listen to an unqualified spoofer. The man in the front row who started off drifting into a doze is now in a deep snoring sleep, getting intermittent belts in the ribs from his embarrassed wife: I'm just grateful there's one less audience member listening. I stutter my way to an uninspired finish and relish the pints of cider and curry chips after. A writer I meet at a festival later that year tells me he saw a photo of me from that event and that I looked terrified.

After the interview, some people come up to get copies of my book signed. A teenager tells me he identifies as a changeling because he doesn't fit in; this happens a couple more times at different events with various teenagers. I ache for them, remembering my own awkward adolescence, and think how wonderful it is they can meet like-minded people online.

A friend invites me to her book group to discuss *Eggshells*. When I arrive, the small talk dribbles away and the women look expectantly at me. We totter around the outskirts of a conversation until I tell them to be honest, they don't have to like the book, I won't be offended. Gradually a discussion gets going about my character Vivian's approach to life. One woman feels very strongly that Vivian has a psychological or neurological condition and that this condition should be treated or at least stated. I say Vivian has no condition I know of, but this isn't satisfactory and the reader heatedly and repeatedly asks what's wrong with her. A psychiatrist in the group says calmly that Vivian can live on her own, she's not a danger to herself or others, she has eccentricities but she's fine. What an incomparable, impossible-to-describe feeling, to sit back and listen to other people having strong opinions about someone you invented. I want to bring this expert reader around with me to interviews from now on and have her do the talking.

THE MUSICIAN PAUL NOONAN EMAILS ASKING ME to write something for a celebration of Dublin Port in the National Concert Hall. I google him and discover he's the lead singer in the band Bell X1. He had read a piece I'd written for *The Irish Times* about a period of unemployment leading to writing my first novel and invited me on the strength of it. What joy – to realise that a piece of honesty has connected with someone. I meet Paul, who is curating the event, and the programme manager, to hear what's involved. They explain the brief: to write something about Dublin Port and to perform the piece, set to music, in front of 1,200 people over three nights. I say I'd love to write the piece but could someone else perform it? They look doubtful. I eventually agree to conquer my nerves, silently imagining three nights of Xanax, and promise to perform.

I love ports and their busyness, so writing about Dublin Port is undaunting: the challenge will be to not go too deep into the research. I don't accomplish this, I wade full-throttle into the history of the port, stories of the dockers, the changing maps of the area, the names of ships, tide timetables, mentions of the Liffey in fiction and nonfiction.

This is how I operate. I get into a subject or project and come at it from all angles and put so many hours of research into it – reading Joyce's *Finnegans Wake* for instance, all the hours that took and getting two phrases from it for my piece (bulgic porterhouse barge; rivering, hitherandthithering waters). I take a boat trip from the river to Dún Laoghaire just to get a glimpse of the port from the water, from a different angle. I visit the National Maritime Museum. I buy books on Dublin Port and Liffey bridges and Liffey ship-building and shipwrecks around the Irish coast; I buy not only *Finnegans Wake* but two books of criticism that help me to understand it. It doesn't occur to me to stop spending so much money and time on a project, I'm all in. It's not a viable way to work. If I had no mortgage or bills, I could live like a nineteenth-century gentleman intellectual but it doesn't work in my century with my monthly outgoings.

At the launch of the concert, Starboard Home, I get talking to a man called John with a white beard who writes poetry. We chat about writing and hearing his accent, I ask, Are you a Dub, John? He laughs. You could say that, he says, I'm one of The Dubliners. I'm mortified, I've been unwittingly talking to the famous John Sheahan.

The musicians I meet during rehearsals are incredibly welcoming and kind, explaining their instruments and their songwriting process. I get given tickets to see The Gloaming at the concert hall and go with my partner, delighted with our front-row seats. As the lights go down, a group shuffles into the seats beside me, one of them looks familiar and as he sits down a couple of seats away, I lean forward to get another gawk, he catches me looking and smiles. I sit back and whisper to my partner, I know that lad, I think he was in my web design FÁS course in Finglas the year I was unemployed. My partner shakes his head wearily. That's Cillian Murphy, he says.

I write my piece and attend a practice session with the National Concert Hall house-band in a studio a few days before the concert. They are putting music to my words, something so thrilling I never even thought to imagine it. Some of the band members are household names; even I have heard of them. After they warm up – tune up? – I'm told, okay Caitríona, you come in when you hear the bass. Bass. What the hell is a bass? I look furtively at each musician and what they're standing or sitting in front of: which one could be the bass? I use process of elimination – it's not the keyboard but there's a guitar and drums and I know there can be bass guitars and bass drums. I remember the line from the children's song 'Big Bass Drum' and these drums don't look very big so I decide on guitar. The rest of the session is me grinning gormlessly, offering no input or feedback when I'm asked for it except a breathless, It all sounds great! I'd love to be able to fake an opinion when one seems to be required.

The concerts go well. I am knee-knockingly nervous, which is visible because the audience is at my feet (not metaphorically, the concert hall slopes downwards) but I even enjoy it. On the last night, the performers all gather in the wings together before going out to take a bow and I look around at these singers all giddy and messing, trying to make each other laugh, like the camaraderie after a cross-country race with your team-mates before a medal ceremony and I think, *This is happiness.*

I'm asked to send an invoice. I go to Easons, buy a book of carbon copy invoices, fill out Invoice Number 001, and send it off by post. I get a very kind email requesting an electronic invoice.

I perform this port piece at Electric Picnic. It means free tickets for myself and my partner for the weekend. I'm elated. I meet another writer there with her children: we agree it's so rare and incredible to be able to bring something from our writing to the household. It's only when Paul Noonan starts the intro that I realise this does not sound the same as the concert hall, there isn't a full band performing and I have no idea when to come in on, Pavlov's dog missing the prompt to salivate. It doesn't go well. The audience is not here to listen to some random woman banging on about a port for eleven long minutes. I decide it's too long for young people at a festival who are there to get hammered and gawk at musicians so I drop paragraphs as I go, which messes up the sense of the piece and the timing of the music. I'm also distracted by an older man stretched horizontal at the side of the tent, hopefully asleep. I race to the end of the piece, willing it to be over, drawing to a poorly timed finish. There may have been some in the crowd who were quietly enjoying it but it's the bored ones looking at their phones I focus on.

'Don't work too hard, you get no thanks for it and more is expected of you' is a constant refrain in cleaning work. How hard I work, how well I clean is up to me. I do sometimes question my insistence on hoovering to perfection the office of someone who is never anything but perfectly ignorant to me. Like Melville's character Bartleby's reply when asked to do some work, 'I would prefer not to,' which became a statement of resistance, I answer some 'Could you just …' requests with a mildly apologetic, 'No, I'm sorry I can't.' I'm not assured enough to use the British royal family's strategy of never apologise, never explain. I don't do extras that morph into expectations, unless they're once-offs for decent people in a bit of a bind.

When my first novel, *Eggshells*, was being sent out, a big publisher expressed tentative interest, on condition that I change the book to include a love story or otherwise conventional ending. I found that grimly cynical and refused to engage: my character was completely self-contained and had no interest in a relationship. But I've since thought that maybe there's a different commercial writing life out there in which I straighten out the quirks of my character, and give them the wedding to end all weddings.

I used to clean a large open-plan office with lots of postgraduate students working in it. One particular postgrad would come in very early, the only person in the whole office. The first morning I approached his desk to empty his bin, I smiled and said good morning. He didn't look up from his computer. I thought he might be hard of hearing so I said it louder. He still didn't look up. I figured he must be extremely shy or socially uneasy so I left him at it, cleaning around him day after day as if I (or maybe he?) were invisible. Then one morning a spare and I were put spring-cleaning the stairwells together. I was on my hunkers cleaning the glass pane of a stairwell door. Although I was clearly visible through the glass, this man barged through the door, knocking me and my bucket of water over. He appeared not to notice and walked on. My co-worker helped clean up the spill; he'd done the same thing to her previously. We talked about telling someone, but how could we prove he'd done it on purpose? Whose word is more valuable, a cleaner's or a postgrad's? Then I saw him one morning, walking with a professor. The postgrad was chuckling arse-lickingly heartily at the professor's joke, adding his own remarks in a jocular voice. There were no hearing issues, no shyness, no social anxiety. That same professor, a kindly man who knew the cleaners by name, told me later how nice this postgrad was. I could only nod, my version wouldn't be credited.

(Is it possible that cleaners have secret unofficial methods of revenge?)

I do an event in a Cork library in which the panellists on-stage outnumber the audience members. The organisers are embarrassed and apologetic, explaining that this talk with newbie unknowns clashes with an event with an established local. I don't mind, especially since I'm with other writers. It can be laughed through. And the hotel has one of the best buffet breakfasts I've ever had; I nearly cause myself a mischief on the way back to Dublin on the bus, I've drunk that many smoothies.

Some mornings I have coffee and toast before I leave work, then I go to the library to work at the novel. Drafting talks and short pieces has taken priority over the manuscript. Because I'm uneasy with public speaking, I put huge effort into preparing for events, even if it doesn't always pay off. I find it hard to sit undistractedly and hack at a long-term goal of a second book with no publisher interest but I force myself. I give my character R an obsession with German compound nouns because I loved them in secondary school.

I found German grammar difficult, its verb forms and the sixteen different instances of which form of the word 'the' to use was a pain in the hoop, but the compound nouns I loved. I liked their Lego-ish ways, piecing individual nouns together to make something that gave off more of a sense of meaning than if you'd made up a new word.

There's *Erbsenzahlen*, which means pea-counting, which means obsessed with details.

And *Mundraub*, which means mouth-grab, which means stealing food from someone's mouth.

I like *Spassmacher*, which means fun-maker, which means clown.

The literalness appeals to me, the need for a double translation, first of the literal words then of the sense of it. I find my old Leaving Cert notebook with lists of handwritten German compound nouns and make lists from those. Then, I use my old German–English dictionary from school and buy a couple more from charity shops (I seem to believe that different dictionaries will contain different words, that the perfect German compound noun will be the key to unlocking the novel). Then, in the National Library reading room, I take the enormous German–English dictionary from the reference shelves and work my way through it. At home I look online for more compound nouns. That is to say, all the hours of cumulative effort I spend scouring dictionaries and obsessing over German compound nouns produces thirty-nine words for my novel.

The Irish Times publishes an article about the publisher of my first novel, stating that they haven't been paying royalties to writers or wages to staff. Having an agent has protected me from some of these issues, I haven't been treated as badly as some other writers so I can't speak publicly on it. I privately discuss my experiences to upcoming writers looking to get published, while watching every word in case they do push ahead with this publisher. Issues of pay might explain why my book is not finding its way into bookshops, why there are problems along the distribution chain. I hadn't heard the whispers two years ago when I was in talks with this publisher; I was too new to the book scene to have access to grapevine wisdom.

I feel foolish now about my naivety. The staff who worked at the publisher were exceptional, working so hard to put books out there and promote them. The publicity surrounding it adds more stress to an already nasty situation; I'm suddenly popular to milk for a scoop.

When the article is published, I'm in a hotel. I have booked myself into a three-star hotel for three nights with huge amounts of snacks to force myself into a non-distractable environment to write my second novel. I've taken a day off work to bulk up my writing time. I'm hoping for a big push that will show me how to salvage this chaos of chronology and character-building. I hide the remote so I'm not tempted by daytime TV shows. I arrange my snacks on shelf. I sit at the desk and stare at the wall under the TV: nothing. I take to the bed and arrange the printed pages of the novel-so-far on the duvet and stare out the window: nothing. I check my phone, texts and emails are coming through about the publisher exposé, some requests for my side of the story. I try so hard to push this from my mind and focus on getting something written: I've paid for this hotel, I need to use this time to get some real work done. I get almost nothing done.

A MONTH LATER, I'M SICK AS A DOG AND HAPPY AS a clam; I'm pregnant. My partner and I decide to go the old-fashioned way and tell nobody until after twelve weeks. It's hard trying to hide the rushes to the bathroom to vomit. In the area I clean, a conference room has grubby lino that needs buffing after events. The buffer machine is heavy and difficult to manoeuvre, and there are strict warnings not to use it when pregnant – even if it doesn't go berserk and upend you, the handles can smash into your belly, giving an awful knock. I make various excuses for three months, letting the lino go dull and listless.

I walk to work, stopping at various points to puke. When I clock in at the security desk pale and shook, the security guards joke that I've been on the whiskey the night before, but as it continues morning after morning, they smile knowingly. The cleaners tell me I'm awful washy looking, I need to eat more fruit, build myself up. When I clean the toilets, strong smells of waste and chemicals attack my hypersensitive sniffers and set me heaving. There's something inefficient about cleaning a toilet, puking in it, and having to clean it again. Bins set me off: yesterday's curry cartons and half-eaten burritos send me hurling back into their depths. I keep moving, I'm in a very busy area and stopping isn't really an option. By the time I'm done dry-retching, I feel a hunger so ravenous I start looking at every unmoving thing as a potential food source. I've never been fussy about food, but now the smell of certain foods has me heaving and hurling; it seems apt they're sporting verbs, it certainly felt like an endurance sport at times. I miss the spontaneity that comes with not being constantly sick, I always pack a plastic bag in an easy-to-access pocket. On a particularly bad day, I bring the bag or basin from room to room. When I go somewhere new, I scout out the toilets and the nearest exit, like an over-cautious airline passenger or pyrophobe. I've legged it the length of a church at a christening to puke, I've begged drivers to let me off buses between stops to hurl on footpaths, I've sprinted up the escalator out of the basement in H&M to vomit on the path outside. Even if I'd been clutching an armful of unpurchased clothes, I reckon the security guard would have left me to my own regurgitary devices.

I've always loved the smell of tarmac but now I can't get enough of it. I find myself crouched down pretending to tie my shoelace at a roadworks as near to a road paver as I can get, poking my head under the barrier to sniff the fresh tarmac.

Things I've found when cleaning:

- Pens.
- Coins.
- A laptop.
- Piss in a bin.
- Piss in a lecture-room sink.
- Condoms (used and unused: in lecture rooms, disabled toilets).
- Vodka bottles (empty, in disabled toilet).
- Gin bottles (empty, in disabled toilet: this is the party toilet).
- Detailed hand-drawn diagrams of various bikini wax styles.
- Fingernail cuttings in offices, labs, libraries (at least I hope they were fingernails).
- Facial hair shavings + disposable razor blade (under desk in library).
- A note in capital letters honking of desperation: SEND NUDES.

Deciding to have a child is the first time in my life I've taken on responsibility, I've flitted from job to travel to job, avoiding being in charge of anyone or anything. Throughout secondary school I loved biology, was fascinated by all things hospital, and applied to study medicine in college, but the night before the change-of-mind application deadline I wiped medicine from my top choice because I realised I couldn't handle being responsible for someone's life. I studied speech and language therapy for two years before dropping out. I loved the range of modules on the course – linguistics, phonetics, psychology, physiology, anatomy, the mix of medical and linguistic. I loved anatomy best, the Friday sessions with human cadavers and the reluctance to eat chicken after seeing the yellowy, chickenish texture of the corpses. We studied head, neck and chest and neuroanatomy and I remember the dark giddiness of being around so much death. We would get attached to particular body parts: this person had a fine set of lungs, that brain was in great shape. The week we studied the circulatory system had us walking from cadaver to cadaver looking for the perfect heart singing Feargal Sharkey's 'A Good Heart'. Medical and dental students dissected the bodies and speech therapy students handled the body parts and studied them afterwards. It was a mindfuck to come in one Friday to see that a body that had been intact the previous week was now sliced down the middle. It was the closest I came to fainting, the realisation after all the joking and tar-dark humour that a human had been sliced lengthways like a sausage on a breakfast roll.

I dropped out of speech therapy because I realised I couldn't cure or fix the children and adults we were put working with in hospital and clinical settings. Improving speech and language issues took so much dedication and time, which often just wasn't available. I couldn't manage to piece together all the theory into figuring out how to get a parent and child living in challenging conditions to practise their sounds when there were more pressing issues to deal with, and I despaired of being motivated enough to do this year on year. My expectations turned to disillusionment and frustration, especially with cruelly long waiting lists: when a child did eventually get seen by a speech therapist, they got just thirty minutes a week. The responsibility of being the go-to person felt crushing. It was too much for me.

I've avoided jobs with responsibility and power. I seek out sheep, not shepherd, roles. I've hunted for jobs based on having the freedom to do my own thing outside of working hours while taking a pay cheque every week. This is why, like my character Vivian in *Eggshells*, I used to search job sites using the key word 'assistant'. As I had Vivian say, 'I don't have a skill at anything but maybe I could assist at something.' Having a baby would be a massive change, I couldn't drift through life any more.

(I would also like a job pushing a trolley. Anything could be on that trolley: medicines, tea and biscuits, cleaning supplies, corpses. I feel it would lend me gravitas and give me something to do with my hands.)

I'm signed up to appear on a panel at a writing festival. The morning of the event, I get up at 4.40 a.m., walk to work, stopping at Des Kelly Carpets in Phibsboro to upend my stomach contents. A woman who walks to work at the same time stops to ask if I'm okay. I give her a thumbs up behind my back, holding my hair back with my other hand. I do my morning's work feeling more wretched than usual and go home, trying to prepare for my event. I can't settle, the sickness is too much. I realise there's no way I can get two buses across the city at rush hour and then sit through an hour-and-a-half on stage without a bucket beside me. I cancel on the pretext of a vomiting bug, feeling bad for the no-show.

I attempt Twitter. I'm not the most tech-savvy and am a very late adopter. I got my first phone in 2009, years after most people, and held out against smartphones for another decade. When I was in college in the early 2000s I was unfamiliar with email. One day my younger sister chanced past as I was finishing an email on the family desktop to a lecturer about meeting him to discuss an essay. She stopped me before I hit send, I was signing off 'Love, Caitríona'. I've since learnt to hold back on the intimacy on official emails but on Twitter, I can't find the right balance between asking people to buy my book/read my article and craven neediness. Like sending a group email, I struggle to pitch at different people, I'm too honest in some tweets or mess up the tone: light-heartedly teasing a friend comes across as just plain mean if you don't know the relationship and context. I also dislike how being on Twitter turns every piece of my life into potential fodder for a tweet, shaping my thoughts and parcelling my experiences into tweet-sized chunks. And as for the lies, I couldn't get beyond hearing people backbiting about writers' successes they felt were undeserved, then tweeting fawning compliments. No, I need a simpler life. I don't do a dramatic Twitter exit, just fade out with a pinned tweet containing my email address.

When I meet a busy person, say a mother of several children who has a successful career and seems to be managing to do many things well, I want to ask her: how often do you wash your towels? People claim to change their bedding fairly frequently but towels dry clean bodies so there isn't the same pressure to claim towel hygiene. (I wash mine when they start to smell.)

In early clandestine pregnancy, I'm invited to a book festival in Italy. It's my first time being invited abroad to talk about my work and I can't believe my luck. I'm sent the general topics and questions in advance by the moderator who's interviewing me at one event. He seems to have interpreted my novel as a communist manifesto, a kind of anti-capitalist diatribe. While I agree with some parts (delightedly, having never thought them out for myself before) I rein him in on others, thinking it a case of adding ingredients to a cake after it's been baked. It shows me that how books are read can have little to do with what the writer intended. I meet other more seasoned writers, some of whom are jaded by the travelling to festivals and staying in different hotels. I find it hard to imagine doing this so often that it's jading,

I'm at the giddy-with-gratitude stage. (A hotel room! Buffet breakfast! ITALY!)

Sometimes the small things trip you up more than the big ones. I soon realise that with pregnancy sickness, Italian dinners are going to be a problem. Meals are endurance tests, the smells of Tuscan stews and pastas that I'd normally gobble up are turning my stomach. I learn to deal with wine pressure: the bottles are left open on the tables so I let someone pour the first round, then grab the bottle and keep refilling others' glasses. Nobody notices my wine glass hasn't been emptied or refilled.

I'm scheduled to do an interview alongside Catherine Dunne, who is something of a celebrity in Italy. She's warm and articulate, a pro at these things. I'm wretchedly tired, and on the way to an event, get a coffee to try and rev myself up. The coffee is tiny, very strong, and my heart starts to race. I get the sweats, waves of it, and retch the whole way to the conference centre. The lecture theatre is huge with large steps down to the front, and it's packed. Fans of Catherine have filled the seats and are starting to crowd the steps, I pick my way down. Since I've been pregnant-puking I carry a plastic bag with me at all times and scan every room for the quickest exit. This theatre has no open doors at ground level to escape through, and the stairs are so crowded that getting through them to race to the toilets would be impossible. I've left my bag with my partner and can't get to my sick bag. I sit sweating beside Catherine, my dripping forehead and anguished expression conveying a high state of nervous anxiety. I get through it: having a generous, more experienced writer beside you is calming.

I have a separate, solo interview about my book and steer the conversation away from socialism and communism, even though the interviewer's interpretation seems reasonable, because I don't have the political know-how to answer them properly. In this as in all interviews, I just want to say I wrote a book about a woman who interested me, that's it. There's no more to it.

I sometimes struggle in situations where an instant opinion is solicited. In tutorials while studying English in university, then as a writer on panel discussions I frequently just don't have an opinion. If I have enough to say about something, I can work up the courage to say it, but when someone comes back with a counter-argument, I can see their point and not only can I not remember or figure out how to defend my point, I often start agreeing with the opposing point. It's for this reason that I don't get involved in reviewing or critiquing work. Years ago, when workshopping other writers' work in my creative-writing class, I struggled to pinpoint the flaws that seemed obvious to others. I'm ill-suited to parts of a professional writing life.

When I do a reading from my first novel and discuss the ideas behind it (belonging, changeling mythology, loneliness, friendship), occasionally questions veer into topics like the advantages and disadvantages of labelling children with autism spectrum disorder. I know so little about them that I don't have an opinion on them and I pick over my words, trying not to misspeak. I explain repeatedly that my main character, Vivian, sees things differently but that I didn't research any kind of neurological or psychiatric condition, I just wrote the world as seen through this particular character's eyes. I'm pressed many times, by interviewers and readers, to diagnose her, to just say what's wrong with her as if I'm keeping some kind of secret from them. I don't see a problem with Vivian's view of the world (possibly because it's similar to how I see the world, just taken to extreme) and my vagueness irritates those who need definites.

The heart-sink of going to clean a toilet when the lid is closed. What horrors lie beneath.

I crave the cold sourness of oranges, devouring whole nets of them, a methodical savagery to my greed. My yearnings are very precise: tinned grapefruit, not fresh; tinned peaches, not fresh. I crave egg mayonnaise sandwiches on white sliced bread. I develop a deep fixation with potatoes, fantasising about them by day and dreaming about them by night. I consider writing an ode to the floury glory of potatoes, skins laughing off. I buy specific recipe books for potatoes and spend hours online researching the best way to roast them. (I rarely get around to doing any of this potato-cooking, the longing is mostly theoretical.) I take temporary notions too, fixating on something for a week then taking against it, the fridge full of half-eaten longings. I salivate over ice and sand. Whenever I get near a beach, I scrabble at the sand, cram it into my mouth, crunch down. I desire this salty grittiness like nothing else, drooling over photos of beaches with hard, damp sand. Like any craving, the first mouthful is heavenly, alleviating something in me.

When I tell my co-workers that I'm pregnant, the response is joyous. News spreads and various cleaners visit my area, offering help and imparting wisdom. One cleaner asks what my longings are. I tell her about the eggs and oranges, thinking it prudent not to mention the sand. Another cleaner looks bewildered and asks what we mean. I explain, assuming our English isn't translating, but no. This woman experienced her pregnancies in rural Yugoslavia in the 1970s. She didn't understand the concept of cravings because they couldn't be satisfied even if she'd felt them. How self-indulgent of me, banging on about having to have this and needing that.

Things other cleaners have found:

- People sleeping overnight in buildings (more frequently since the housing crisis).
- The son of a professor having sex with a woman on the swivel chair in his father's office. What level of Oedipal issues would you have to want to ride someone on your dad's work chair? And how much core strength would it take to counter the chair's swivel and hold your thrust?

I don't buy pregnancy books and politely decline when women offer me theirs. Our house contains thousands of books: any possible wall-space holds books; piles of books are used as makeshift shelves; I'm constantly thinking of ways to throw out things so I can have more room for books. But books for me are for fantasy, escape, enjoyment, not for instructive facts. The internet is for information. Every week I look up a pregnancy website to find out what's happening inside me, what fruit or ball shape the embryo/foetus is, and what I should be at. I skip ahead for the watermelon-sized foetus but we're all pretending it won't come to that.

Some mothers ask if I'm going to follow a certain method or approach, in familiar first-name terms: have you tried Gina, are you doing baby-led/attachment parenting. The only books I read about parenthood are the non-prescriptive ones by writers who reflect on their experience without preaching, the memoirs saying this was my experience, it will not necessarily be yours. How can parents rear babies so certainly, according to methods and practices and schemes, how does that work? I assumed that nobody would know my babies because they hadn't been here before; I would learn about them as they became themselves. This seemed an outlandish way to approach parenthood to some, as if I thought I knew everything. I didn't. I knew that I knew nothing but I also knew that everyone else knew nothing about this baby.

A sink in a lecture room has a leak in the pipe underneath. I put a bucket under the sink to catch the dirty leak-water. One morning I find myself distractedly pouring the dirty water from that bucket down the sink only to have to thrust the bucket back into place to catch it as it leaked out the pipe. The House that Jack Built.

After hearing the communist interpretation of *Eggshells*, I come across an academic journal article that suggests my character Vivian uses changeling legend to embody a nonconforming gender presentation, that she looks to queer models of kinship. It's thrilling to read interpretations of my work in ways I never thought of, but seem perfectly valid. Vivian feels even more real to me then. In a readers' guide to *Eggshells*, I learn that my character's obsession with sweets and treats, skipping meals to focus on cake, is an arrested development, an attempt to revert to childhood. But ... this is the one way in which my character and I are in total accord: I think constantly about treats, and will always choose junk food over meals. This is a psychological analysis of me. I'm intrigued by the certainty of these interpretations of a text and feel fortunate to be long enough in the tooth to not take them personally, while being flattered by the fact that my character sparks such serious evaluation. I'll listen to my doctor and my dentist about my fancy for sweet treats, happy to ignore anything else.

The word 'gauche' is used pejoratively. It's never meant as a good thing. I like gauche, I'm drawn to such people. Gauche is natural and honest, not putting on a fake persona, but we're supposed to prefer over-confident, showy bluster.

I google maternity clothes. I can't justify spending money on clothes I won't use much so I buy some leggings with expanding waistbands and baggy tops that I can use after. On a clothing website I see a 'maternity milkmaid dress', which seems a bit premature.

I HEAR FROM A FRIEND THAT A POSITION HAS opened up in the museum building. I'm ensconced in the arts block and have my routine sorted, but the pull of the old building is strong. And the floor I'd be going into in the museum building has no toilets to clean, which, in my hypersensitive-sniffer state, would be a relief. I'd be swapping easy-to-clean lino and tiles for crumbling paintwork and warped wooden floors, giving up the use of a lift for many staircases, but it feels like coming home. And with fewer conferences, I can plan around the big jobs and not just react to requests. I can get properly stuck in on my own terms. My supervisor is aghast, I've to convince her that I'll take the stairs handy – she's possibly imagining a compo claim from a pregnant fall – but stairs are easier to manage than the bin bag-lugging in the arts block. (One morning I filled sixteen clanking, bulging bin bags after a particularly gregarious conference.)

A cleaner in the building I move to is unimpressed, glaring at my belly and snarling that I'll be gone on maternity leave soon and then where'll they be. She has a point. There's something quite refreshing about open hostility. Grievances can be aired more openly in the housekeeping world, information is demanded honestly: how much did you pay for your house? How much is your weekly pay? I settle in, find my 'office' to hide in between tasks, make my own of the cubby.

I have three hoovers on three different level floors in this area. One of them, the hoover in a library up a rickety, bockety, windy staircase that creaks and wobbles with every step, is held together with masking tape. Some days, happiness is the hoover pipe not falling off, requiring me to bend over and fix it and grip it in place as I hoover. The cleaners I worked with fifteen years ago, who are retiring or retired, describe cleaning in an era before health and safety guidelines, when they lugged hoovers up and down flights of steps, scrubbed stone steps on their knees. Some have debilitating back, hip, knee, shoulder problems; the joints are not impressed.

The decency of maintenance crew, attendants and cleaners when I'm pregnant: I can't leave a bin bag down only for it to be grabbed and taken downstairs for me. Buckets of water for washing stairs are yanked from my hand, Give me that, let me do that. When I come in shaky and nauseous at

6 a.m., the 5 a.m. cleaners on their break wait to microwave their breakfast eggs until I've gone upstairs to my area. On days I'm very ill, I lumber up three flights of steps to the drawing office, an attic double lecture room. It has shiny wooden floors that are cool and smooth and oh-so-soothing to lie on. I stretch out, manoeuvring into position so my forehead touches the cold hard floor, I hold a bin bag to my mouth and prop myself up on my elbow to puke, then lie back down between bouts, the cold floor a gorgeous relief to my sweaty forehead. Recovery is quick and I'm back up, flying around with my bin bag, ravenously thinking of when I can eat and what I can eat and how much of it. An office I clean has a water cooler: tiny sips of ice-cold relief.

My job involves assessing: whether a dustpan and brush, for example, is enough to get rid of a few crumbs, or whether it needs a full hoover. Since pregnancy I've been asking myself: what can I get away with? Used to be, I'd spend ages cleaning something that wouldn't be noticed. I would turn desks upside down like sheep turned turtle and hack at the encrusted chewing gum with a metal scraper; now I put my back pain and energy levels first. 'You get no thanks for it' has sunk in.

I have my babies late: my co-workers had theirs early, they've managed to squeeze in another generation more than I have. I'm an anomaly in the housekeeping department, an Irish woman in her late thirties of willingly reproductive years. The other 200 cleaners are mostly either older Irish women near retirement age, or women and men in their twenties and early thirties from other countries, either having settled in Ireland or just passing through on a jaunt: from Mexico, Mauritius, Poland, Latvia, Lithuania, China, Nigeria, Serbia, England, Russia, Brazil. There are many young Brazilians working in housekeeping while studying English and often working another job to keep up with Dublin rents. Fifteen years ago, when I was cleaning in Trinity, there were lots of young Chinese cleaners, working part-time while studying English. They usually adopted English names, some picking footballers' or celebrity names, one couple unwittingly taking on the names of a couple from *Coronation Street*. The notion of choosing another name, another identity, fascinated me and I wondered if they behaved differently in a different name. I didn't have to adopt a Japanese name when I lived in Japan; the Japanese made the effort to pronounce my name. Hurricane Katrina happened while I was there, some of my students started calling me Typhoon.

There are cleaners who identify with hoarders, and cleaners who itch to get in and clear it all away. I'm the former, I understand the resistance to discarding all the hard-won knowledge, the layers of learning. We're told firmly never to discard anything that's not actually in the bin; cleaners have on occasion thrown away piles of paper flung higgledy-piggledy near a bin that turned out to be exam scripts.

Cleaning the offices of lecturers who keep everything is much easier than cleaning those of more pernickety staff members whose offices are so scrupulously arranged I'm afraid to touch anything for fear of disturbing or dirtying it. One lecturer I cleaned for had a huge office filled with papers and books in dothery towers. There was a narrow goat-path to the desk, the legs of which were the only things that met the carpet: the chair and bin were balanced precariously on knee-high slopes of papers. I looked forward to 'cleaning' this room because all I could do was empty the bin. The goat-path was too narrow to even attempt to hoover without causing a paper avalanche.

Another lecturer had just a square patch of paper-free carpet in front of their desk, the rest was piles of books and papers. I hoovered that small square meticulously, feeling like someone polishing the decks of the *Titanic* as it sank.

I'VE GOT A DEAL WITH A SMALL NEW YORK PRESS to publish *Eggshells*, which came about in the most beautifully serendipitous way. A San Francisco bookseller stumbled upon a used copy of my novel and sent it to his friend Dennis who runs Melville House in Brooklyn. Dennis got in touch with my Irish publisher and asked about rights. The way these things happen is thrilling and terrifying, how close they come to not happening, how *chancy*. The publisher invites me over to the Winter Institute event in Minneapolis to meet booksellers, followed by a few days in Brooklyn with publishing and library people. Being given a trip overseas will never not feel exhilarating.

The morning I fly to the US in January 2017 is the first day of Trump's infamous Muslim ban. Security is tighter and meaner. In the queue to check in at Dublin Airport, an official questions why I'm flying to the US. I hand him my printed-out itinerary and explain that I'm a writer attending a bookselling conference. He asks what I've written, why I need to go to the US. I try to answer his questions but nausea is escalating and I'm starting to sweat. He looks closely at me and asks why I appear anxious. I'm five months pregnant, I say, and I'm concentrating on not vomiting. He quickly hands back my itinerary and moves away; nothing scares a man so much as a pregnant woman liable to leak from either end. At US security pre-clearance, the queue moves slowly: men with brown skin are being taken into rooms for questioning. The official wants to know what kind of writer I am. A novelist, I say. He looks blank. I write fiction, I say – thinking officials might regard making things up as journalism's less scary cousin. (When I travelled to Iran years ago, I invented an admin job for myself so I wouldn't have to put the dread-word abstract writer on my visa application.) The immigration officer looks at me: Ma'am, will you be writing your novel fictions in America? No sir, I say. Something about the formal politeness of Americans at work appeals to me, and I step up my sirs and ma'ams.

I have dinner with my publisher and his assistant in Minneapolis after two flights in which I make full use of the sick bags, not helped by the suited men beside me sniggering about which of their au pairs and cleaners are the most fuckable. The publishing assistant is young and enthusiastic, full of fizz. He talks excitedly about the events of the next few days, including a yoga session at six o'clock the next morning. I've been awake for almost twenty hours at this point,

I can't even formulate an excuse. Over the next few days I meet bookstore owners and book people. It's a relief to be openly pregnant; people are understanding about a sudden bathroom sprint or opting out of late-night karaoke sessions to Cinderella myself to bed at midnight. In between events I arrange to hang out with another debut author. She says she has work to do first. What work, I ask, wondering if I should be doing some prep for these meet-and-greet events. She looks strangely at me, Writing, she says, I'm working on my next book. Oh that. I realise that I too should be using the downtime built into my schedule to work on my second novel, but that couldn't be further from my head so I watch TV on the huge bed or explore the ferociously cold downtown, soon realising that the only other people out walking are furiously unstable or high on various substances, or both. There is concern among the Americans later when I tell them of my adventures: you walked where, alone?

I go to New York to meet the publishing staff and librarians. Attending a meeting in the midtown office of the book distributor, looking out the window at skyscrapers, I feel like Carrie Bradshaw in *Sex and the City*, trying to suppress the giddy. I'd spent a summer in New York when I was 20, drinking in bars using a fake ID from a cousin who looked nothing like me. That summer I applied unsuccessfully for jobs in shops and cafés in Manhattan, considered egg donation that paid a medium fortune – $5,000 in 1999 (too young, had to be 21) – or volunteering for 'investigational drug experiments' (even at 20 I suspected this might not be wise for my long-term health). I opted to work as a carer, doing a week-long carers' course in which I learnt how to take a glass eye out and clean the eye socket, detach a false leg, insert catheters into rubber urethras, wash rubber models of genitals – the instructor shouting DON'T FORGET BETWEEN THE BUTT CHEEKS. Thankfully I didn't have to carry out all of these tasks in my real work. Now, eighteen years later, I visit Tompkins Square Park in the East Village, to look at the tiny studio apartment (an illegal sublet) facing the park where three of us crammed onto a double mattress and sofa cushions we found on the street.

The earlier I get up (if I'm up before my alarm, sick), the later I end up in work. I busy myself with sending emails, trying to remember to schedule Send for 8 a.m. or I look like a crackpot obsessive sending wee-hours replies. I get so engrossed in the task that fills my sleepless minutes that I forget to leave the house on time.

Cleaners who have worked decades in Trinity have a flock memory of accumulated knowledge and experience. In the museum building, we talk of the 'red stairs' that have been blue for decades, but to call them anything other than the red stairs in a building full of staircases is to risk confusion. We talk about Terry's office, even though Terry retired years ago. It feels like the theory of monarch butterflies migrating over Lake Superior, reaching a specific point before making a quick turn – thought to be the position of a long-gone looming glacier. My farmer uncle talks of sheep continuing to jump over a stile that is no longer there when they reach a gap in the ditch, the knowledge having been passed down generationally. A much-vandalised phone box is removed from outside a pub near where I live; I find myself skirting around the square patch of footpath where it was, as if it's still there, a ghost box.

When I'm six months pregnant, bathroom renovations begin in my house. The toilet flusher has been held together with wire for years after a drunk friend's over-exuberant flushing, the bath has unscrubbable tractor tyre-mark stains from the previous owner. We'd tried for a long time to get it done, but a big job for us is a small job for builders and our terraced house has no driveway or side entrance or laneway for access. Several prospective builders called to examine the job and left in a hurry promising to call, and never returned. These builders come in, turn off the water, rip out the toilet, bath, basin and then disappear. For three weeks. I pee in a bucket (at the far end of my capacity to squat), shower at my parents' or friends' houses and ease off on liquid intake.

In the back bedroom, the builders have pulled up some floorboards to access radiator pipes, leaving holes in the floor with a gap and then plasterboard to the kitchen below. I start painting this bedroom and for much of the day,

I remember where not to step as I drag around the ironing board holding the paint tray and roller. But when I get tired in the evening, I forget. I back into a hole, crash, I realise I've fallen through the kitchen ceiling and am stuck tight. I look down and see the kitchen tiles beneath me; oh the fright hits me then. My partner tries to hoist me out but I'm top-heavy and well wedged, thigh-deep in plasterboard. I get hysterically giggly, thinking of what this looks like from beneath, a leg dangling through the ceiling. I need a bit of time to gather myself and figure out the angle to manoeuvre my belly out and eventually I get there. I knock back a glass of cold water and this does the trick – the baby kicks and all is well. I text a photo of the hole in the ceiling to the builder; he comes the next day.

A co-worker describes a meeting about car-parking spaces for Trinity staff members. It emerges during the meeting that some cleaners have parking permits. An older, plummy-toned lecturer asks my co-worker later in bewilderment, But how do the *cleaners* have cars?

Seven months into the pregnancy, I feel a sense of low-grade panic about needing to finish the second novel before the baby comes, but it's too hard to write while sick and while the house is in chaos. I can't buy anything for the baby because there are no available surfaces. Everything from the bathroom and one bedroom is stuffed into other rooms; there are boxes of tiles and building materials everywhere else. The builders are guilted into returning after my unintentional sky-diving stunt and they finish the bathroom: relief. Then I slowly, sluggishly paint the house, room by room. The painting itself is soothing and hypnotic, the prepping and the cleaning up after a nuisance. I resort to throwing out brushes to save on chores. I listen to interviews with writers while I'm painting, and yet, inspiring as it is, it doesn't make me sit and write. I have a shark-like need to keep doing and moving; if I stop moving I'll fall asleep. I'm too distracted to get my head back in the novel-in-progress when the priority is having a liveable house.

Eggshells is just out in the US and the publisher has set up twenty-five radio interviews across different states. Many evenings or nights when my brain has virtually checked out with exhaustion, I have a live phone interview on a regional radio station. The interviewers are enthusiastic, but I struggle to perform on fast-paced morning shows with a five-minute slot in which to discuss my book concisely and excitably. I'm advised to correct the interviewers if they get my name or the name of my book wrong, but one radio-show host calls me Lolly for the entire interview and I'm so taken with the loveliness of the word that I forget to correct him, distracted by different-coloured flying lollipops in my head.

A 'gospel and talk station' plays the gospel song 'Nobody Greater' as background holding music while I'm waiting to go on, making me giggle; it reminds me of the nun manning the convent phone in *Father Ted* saying 'Please hold' before belting out the Ave Maria. There are inevitable hiccups: one presenter can't manage the country dialling code for Ireland and blames me for 'not answering', clearly assuming Ireland is an offshoot of the United States. In another interview, the signal is so bad I can mostly hear crackling and fizzing so I just shout random statements about my book, hoping the odd sentence matches up to the question asked. Probably looks like I'm in character as my slightly odd protagonist.

Walking the two miles to work becomes undoable after seven months. The baby is sitting very low so every step hurts. My usual half-hour fast walk now takes forty-five or fifty minutes, with time built in for doubling over in stitch pain and pukes. One morning I'm bent over vomiting at the entrance to a park when a man approaches asking for two euro. He looks jittering-desperate for cash but I don't have any; he gets quite agitated until I tell him I'm pregnant and have no money. His demeanour immediately softens and he offers me a clump of €2 coins from his closed fists. The sheer decency is humbling. I tell him no but thank you so much, feeling the worst kind of disingenuous: my version of no cash on me was nowhere close to his reality. It reminds me of walking home after a night out years ago when a man stepped out of a laneway and demanded my phone. It was too late to run and after a few pints I hadn't the speed of thought to bargain, so I took out my phone and handed it to him, a basic Nokia in the smartphone era. He took one look at the phone and said, Nah you're alright luv and I walked on with my unwanted phone, bathed in the pity of a potential robber.

My inability to move quickly or carry buckets of water, combined with a midwife's orders to do only 'light housework' (which she seemed to mean pootling about with a feather duster), leads me to stop work. I've worked thirty weeks of pregnancy and I need to be off my feet. I am not off my feet. I go after anything that doesn't move with white paint, working at a bovine pace. Third-trimester sickness involves waking suddenly on my back dreaming that someone is strangling me, rushing to sit up grabbing my throat, choking on vomit. My throat is raw from acid-burn, I'm milling into the Strepsils.

The maternity hospital bag list mentions a 'Large, dark-coloured towel' as part of its requirements.

At an antenatal appointment, the midwife says I'll feel a 'stinging sensation' while I'm pushing the baby out, nothing more. There seems to be a conspiracy of silence surrounding labour, if not outright lies. Childbirth is 'discomfort', 'stinging', a 'light burning sensation'. I'd rather truthful information, not candy-coated euphemisms. The pregnancy blogs and websites are so unrelated to my life I've stopped looking at them. For the last month or so, I'm supposed to be resting and putting my feet up. (Nap while you can! See a movie with your husband while you can!) And mild nesting – buying clothes for the baby and prewashing them (why would you bother, why create needless extra work for yourself?) – not the extreme nesting of frantic home improvements.

I am not writing. I can't focus on make-believe characters when a real character-to-be is making its presence felt so insistently inside me: this baby lunges and dives, a barrage of knees and elbows at my insides like a goldfish butting its bowl. Every time I sit down to write and lapse into daydreams or lists of things to be done, I can't help but think of the sheer preciousness of complaining about writer's block. When I worked as an abstract writer I had to write forty-six abstracts a day, 230 a week. I couldn't cry block and sigh at my desk, I had to keep powering through reading those articles and writing those summaries because if I was ten short one day, I'd have fifty-six to write the next. In that job there was a direct correlation between words produced and euro earned; this current novel-writing task is more ambivalent.

We've ordered a new kitchen from Ikea. The bathroom and kitchen needed doing for years, but the rush only came on us just before the baby is born. The money comes from the Dublin Port concert, which paid out more than I've ever earned from writing. I'm going to call it the Starboard Home kitchen, and consider replacing the window with a porthole. The date we're given for the kitchen delivery is the same date as I've been given for the baby's delivery; the actual work will start a couple of days later. This baby better come late. I speed up my painting. I can't sleep for sickness so I'm up at four or five with the June brightness, painting walls, banisters, skirting boards. I stop short at ceilings now, no more wobbles or falls. I have colossal daytime naps in that respite after puking.

At the bus stop, I wait for a bus to go to the maternity hospital for an appointment. A woman arrives and asks when it's due. Five minutes I say, pointing at the screen. Jaysus she says, are they that accurate now? They are, I say, doesn't it make life much easier? She asks if I've time to get to the hospital in five minutes; she meant the baby, not the bus.

We clear all the food from the kitchen, the pots and pans, delph, appliances and accumulated accoutrements. On my due date the new kitchen is delivered. The baby isn't. Added to the chaos of the kitchen contents all over the house are the large boxes containing new kitchen fittings and appliances. I set up camp in the bedroom with a kettle and toaster: the bed is the only free space, and a path I create to the bathroom to puke. We go and buy a pram from Argos for forty euro. It's made by Mattel and looks like a child's toy pram, I'm doubtful it's sturdy enough for a real baby, half-convinced we've bought a toy pram by accident. My partner assembles the pram on the bed, the only available flat space.

I give up on painting. The insides of the bedroom doors remain unglossed, I lie whaled on the bed. The kitchen fitters arrive: there are three lads, the youngest keeps eyeing my bump in obvious fear. They ask how long I have left. I don't tell them I'm overdue for fear of inciting an exodus, I answer vaguely, another few weeks. On the second day, the men work away and I stay upstairs, coming down to answer any questions. On the third day, they say they'll be finished by lunchtime, that's good because I feel very odd.

The first contraction comes, a shocker, like someone hacking a saw across my back and I roar out. One of the men shouts, Are you okay? I shout back yes, I just stubbed my toe. I dutifully start writing down the timing and spacing of contractions, which rip across my lower back. This can't be right, labour is supposed to be in the front. I google it and back labour comes up. It's hell. The worst pain I'd experienced before now is bone breaks and sprains, a tooth abscess, root canal, two fillings with no anaesthetic by a dentist who mistakenly believed I was allergic to numbing fluid. This pain makes those old pains laughable. Back labour is like: something drilling into the nerves at the base of my spine every few minutes.

I get on all fours, roll on the yoga ball, do the breathing but it's hard to not low like a cow when the contractions burn through my back. The men shout up a question and I come downstairs. Which side of the fridge do you want the handle? I don't care, I say, sweating. Are you alright, love, one asks. I'm great, I say, can you decide please? One of them gives a demonstration of the handle being on either side, getting up a monologue about which side makes more sense, which is closer to the kitchen door or too close to other cupboard doors. Another contraction starts. I bend and grip the new counter, suppressing a groan as best I can. Are you sure you're okay, one of them asks nervously. Never better, I say, eyeballing the living daylights out of him. The younger lad begins to look very, very frightened, eyeing my belly as if it's a live bomb. It's okay, just a cramp I say, trying not to roar but unable to suppress a low groan. The left side of the fridge, I say. Are you sure? he asks. That would mean the door opens towards the ... Yes, the left side, I say, and hobble from the room, bent double like a candy cane. But what about the— It's fine, I shout, it's all fine, whatever you think works best. I crawl back upstairs on all fours, bury my face in the duvet for the worst of the contractions and manage to muffle them unnoticed. The men call me down to see the finished kitchen. I've only a few minutes until the next contraction so I thank them quickly and usher them out while they're explaining that the cupboard under the sink didn't have enough space for the shelves we'd ordered. It's fine, it's all fine, it looks great, JUST GREAT, I shout. They look surprised. If you want an undemanding customer, choose a distracted, slightly demented woman in labour.

When they're gone, I hobble around the new kitchen. It feels so strange to not know my outsides when something so alien is happening to my insides. The cupboards are full of sawdust shavings so I get a stepladder and wait for a contraction to come. Once it has subsided, I get up on the stool and clean the drill dust out. I have time to do a shelf before a contraction, another shelf before the next and so on. I obsessively log every contraction and calculate the minutes apart; it's a means to an end, a way to be guaranteed entry to hospital and not be sent home. I'd heard labour described as running a marathon but I've run four marathons and this back pain is a savagery that feels unendurable. I labour through that night with my partner, and the next day at home until eventually, thirty-three hours in, we go to the hospital.

What follows is twenty-three more hours of labour, induced labour now: back-to-back contractions that are like watching the highlights of a football game, with no dead space to recover between excitements. At various points things go tits-up, belly-up, awry in ways I can't keep track of, whispered conversations among staff, over-loud reassurances to me. My vital signs (and/or the baby's?) start to go on the fritz. The oxytocin cannula has been put in wrong, oxytocin has seeped into the tissues and not the vein, the right arm that has been under a blanket is found to be swollen to Shrek-like proportions, so unlike anything resembling a human limb that I get the giggles. Suddenly I become a person of interest: the doctor is brought in, the consultant is summoned, I'm asked why I didn't mention the pain in my arm: because it's nowhere near the pain of labour, I try to explain, I didn't think anything of it. There is an attempt to make me dislodge a stuck baby, a hellish sixty minutes of unproductive pushing. This uncertainty was where I should have stepped in and asked for intervention, put a stop to this madness, but I was a good girl (they call you a good girl when you push) and good girl I was, meekly obedient.

After 55-and-a-half-hours of labouring to nowhere, a siren in the delivery room is sounded, an emergency declared. A porter comes with a trolley and board to manoeuvre me onto it. An anaesthetist appears and injects me, rubbing ice cubes on different parts of my body asking if I could feel this or that; on my other side is a doctor asking me to sign away my womb in case of uncontrollable haemorrhage. I struggle to hold the pen but illegibly sign away my womb. There's a sudden bliss of painlessness, no more back agony, I could fall in love with this anaesthetist.

What follows is: a stuck baby in difficulty, a race to the theatre, a tense silence when I make a light-hearted comment, my realisation that all might not be well. A baby becoming unstuck with a medieval birthing tool, a haemorrhage, a baby rushed for checks, a mother drifting in and out of consciousness. There is straining to see the baby, hearing her cries, unable to reach her. There is a baby put on the mother's chest, a weight like the start of the world.

The next morning, the paediatrician comes to my bedside. You'll have noticed her face is not symmetrical, he says. He's wrong, I'll not have noticed. Her face has wounds and dents from the forceps but she is predictably perfect. How can anyone ask a freshly made mother about imperfection? I stare uncomprehendingly. The diagnosis: facial nerve palsy that will affect the palate and sucking, among other things, and will require months of monitoring and physio. She can't latch onto the breast, she struggles hugely with sucking the bottle. That explains the hazy small-hours intimacies of the previous night: a midwife whisperingly milking me into a tiny dropper and then squeezing it into my fledgling's mouth.

IN THE STRUGGLY MONTHS THAT FOLLOW, I SPEND many hours wondering if the prognosis would have been better if I hadn't been so compliant and begged – no, demanded – safer intervention earlier. It was a needlessly brutal birth. I naively assumed a hideously long labour was only hard on the mother; I didn't factor how risky it was to the child. If I'd been more assertive. If I'd come into hospital earlier in the labour so I could be logged on the system (my labour was only counted as twenty-three hours, from when I arrived into hospital, those thirty-three hours at home have disappeared, were never put on the files). If. If. If.

Later, when I'm attending physio in the maternity hospital for my daughter's tailbone injury and my own tailbone birth injury, I'm told I can request my files and discuss what happened with the doctor who delivered my daughter. I quail. Years later, I still quail at the idea of reading my pain and fear translated into medical jargon, of reliving it and finding the spaces where I could have acted differently and changed the outcome.

The physio pulls out a checklist for birth trauma PTSD and ticks the boxes, tells me there's counselling available from a midwife-turned-counsellor. I balk. I don't want to see midwives again, I want to get beyond the antenatal and birth part of things into the baby part; I want to put the process behind me and focus on the product.

A lawyer friend tells me I have a medical negligence case but I want no case, I feel only gratitude to the doctor who delivered me a live baby. I think of this doctor's visit to my bedside the morning after the birth to ask if I have family living nearby, to tell me I'll be in a lot of pain for a long time and might find the trauma difficult to accept. That's extra, that kindness. It was the system that thwarted us, not an individual; the child and I fell between busy wards, shift changes, and various reluctances to make a decision.

Back home, the public health nurse calls to give the baby her three-day heel prick test. We're in the kitchen; she asks for a bowl of warm water. I can't remember which cupboard the bowls were stuffed back into after the renovation. I'm standing behind the nurse, gesticulating wildly at my partner, mouthing, Where are the bowls? I don't want her to think I'm so befuddled I can't find basic items, can't cope. When the midwife pricks the baby's heel, she screams in pain and fright, I sob and leak milk. It physically hurts me when she hurts. This is something bigger than me, bigger than thinking.

Time both speeds up and slows down. An hourglass in the bedroom has gone wonky, the clumps of sand jamming in the narrowest point until I tap it to release it. It seems symbolic somehow. Two days after I come home from hospital, when I pull up the blinds in the bedroom, it comes as a surprise that there is an outside, that cars and people are going about as usual. All my thoughts and energies are focused not just on the baby but internally, on my body and its pain. Pain deletes my courage, my thinking power, my reasoning ability, which frustrates me. The new kitchen disorients me. Figuring out electrical appliances has never been my strong point, but now I need to understand a dishwasher, hob, microwave, as well as the baby steriliser, amounts for formula-making and work out how to get the baby into the pram and the baby carrier. My partner figures them out and I write myself detailed instructions for each new accoutrement. I've never lived in a house with a dishwasher and think of my grandmothers and how their lives would have been so much easier with it.

Feeding is very difficult. The facial nerve palsy means the baby finds it hard to clamp her mouth on the teat and can only manage a few sips at a time. She can't take in enough to satisfy her, or enough to send her to sleep for any length of time. We feed her near constantly and still her weight drops low, she's on the public health nurse watch-list. She won't sleep for more than twenty minutes at a time; my brain is operating in slow-motion sludge.

One evening we're pushing the baby in her pram, about to cross the road when a group of lads in a car screech past us taking the turn at speed, tyres lifting off the ground, music blasting, cheering, the before in a road traffic safety ad. I still can barely walk, and am conscious of this human that I'm responsible for, her tiny bruised head just feet away from the car. That's my way of excusing what I said next, which is, I wish they'd just die, all of them. My partner is shocked. I'm shocked. I feel a rage I didn't think myself capable of, a visceral hatred. Maybe a more generous version of motherhood would mean I view the boy racers as other people's children, but I just see them as a threat to mine. Before having children, I'd look at a disaster or tragedy on the news and feel sorry for the people involved. Now I link their pain and loss to my own if anything happened to my children; birth has not enlarged me, it has made me more selfish, looking to protect my own.

We hear sirens a lot, living on a main road near a hospital, fire station, garda station. My heart starts racing when I hear the wail of a siren, the exact pitch and rise of the upsurge of her cry. Does it say something about the insularity, my inward-looking version of motherhood when I feel relief that it's a siren, somebody else's problem? I watch *Dunkirk* shortly after the birth. I'm still in terrible pain and cannot connect with the film. Is this heroic? I keep asking. But sitting down isn't agony for him, he only has to save himself, not look after a tiny, helpless creature while in pain. I try watching *Breaking Bad* but find myself weeping for the drug addict who smashes himself into a tree while high. Apparently this is dark comedy but I've lost that part of my sense of humour. Giving birth has made me a combination of skinned-alive sensitive to some kinds of pain and callous to other more celebrated kinds of suffering.

The idea of going back into my old novel now seems outlandish and frankly unreasonable. I do not have cognitive powers for anything else but responding to the baby. And my responses are unpredictable; just weeks ago I would have enjoyed *Dunkirk* and *Breaking Bad*. There's been a rupture in my life, in me, there's a before and an after and I have no idea how to get my brain back to the before. My partner's body and mind are the same, his life is a busier continuation, mine as I knew it is gone.

I'm living on emotion and instinct with no capacity to think out writing challenges. It's baffling to me that only weeks ago, I saw myself as a writer and was thinking about my book, even if I wasn't writing it. The notion of writing my way back into the negative dark space of my novel seems crazed; it's just made up when this baby is real, how could I go back to that world? How can I go back into a novel when I'm no longer that person; I might not be able to focus on make-believe I no longer believe in.

All I can think of is getting enough milk into the baby to get her weight up, take us off the watch-list, get enough milk into her to get her to sleep for more than twenty minutes at a time. I feed her near constantly: she's on the bottle unless she's asleep and she doesn't sleep much.

Close to midnight I do a nappy change and open the front door to put the nappy in the bin. A black cat stands on the doorstep looking expectant and slightly irritated, as if it's been knocking for a while. I leave the nappy bag on the step and open the door wider. The cat marches inside and conducts a haughty tour of the living room before heading into the kitchen. When it's finished strolling the perimeter, I walk upstairs and the cat follows me. I go in and out of bedrooms and the cat comes too, rubbing its face against the walls. I go back downstairs, the cat on my heels, and open the front door. It steps outside and I close the door, wondering whether to read this midnight visitor as a good or bad omen, hoping that at least its scent will deter mice.

Once I'd mastered the quantities of formula and boiling water (and the kitchen appliances and accoutrements to make them) I began to enjoy preparing bottles. It reminded me of the work experience I did as a teenager in a dentist's surgery: making up substances for fillings, developing X-rays, cleaning the blood after extractions. Evenings when I wash bottles, make formula, clean the kitchen, I know I'm supposed to be stilled by the drudgery but I find it satisfying. I like routine jobs through which I can think or listen to music. I like putting cups and plates and cutlery in the correct place; sterilising and preparing bottles. There is an order to this thirty minutes that will break down as soon as I go to bed and the night fragments into multiple parts beyond my control. That said, I'm aware of how much labour my devices save me: my rituals are sterilising bottles in the microwave rather than steeping in fluid, filling and emptying the dishwasher rather than washing up by hand, throwing dirty nappies in the bin rather than washing in buckets. It feels like love in motion.

When I did a women's studies module in transition year in secondary school, the teacher asked what developments or progress did we think was the most significant for Irish women. I said disposable nappies, she wrote that on the blackboard. The next girl said, the right to vote, the next said, the right to work after marriage. I felt embarrassed by my nappies written in chalk beside these huge milestones in women's rights, but now I stand by my choice.

I receive gifts of hand cream from mothers who talk of their dry hands after so many nappy changes. I'm grateful, if a little baffled; my hands are in far better shape from sporadic nappy changes than from hours spent in sweaty rubber gloves, wringing cloths, clasping mop handles.

Every year I buy a large diary. I write things in small daily slots on the left and general to-do lists on the lined page on the right. The year before I have babies, I buy small diaries; there are fewer events and official appointments to fill in, even though the days are busier with smaller tasks that never make it to the diary. In the case of this baby, I didn't predict the sheer number and frequency of medical appointments; she should have had her own diary solely for health matters. She endures thirteen months of medical interventions for the nerve palsy, followed by sporadic appointments for her hips.

We are referred to a hospital dietitian to improve the feeding, get her weight up. The dietitian asks me to log the baby's feeds, the timings and millilitres drunk each time. After three days, she calls and asks me to read out my notes. By the time we've reached 11 a.m. there are twelve feeds done, tiny amounts every time. The dietitian asks me to stop and count how many day and night feeds. That day there are forty-seven feeds in a 24-hour period. I wait to be scolded for doing it wrong/spoiling her/being too nice – all the things I've heard from parents of children who don't have a facial nerve palsy. Instead, she tells me I'm doing a tremendous job in difficult circumstances.

I ask if there's any alternative: it does seem mad now that I see the frequency written down. She says there's no alternative with this particular birth injury; we'll start solids as early as possible – seventeen weeks. The relief that I'm not needlessly complicating things, of being understood by a professional, is immense.

During this period I seek out writings about motherhood, but almost every poem and memoir I find is about the beauty of breastfeeding. I consider writing an essay about the methodical beauty of sterilising bottles and making formula, but I haven't the courage to take on those who view infant formula as arsenic. One night, I happen across Eavan Boland's poem 'Night Feed' and think, Here we go, yet another poem about nursing your baby at the breast and gazing into the baby's eyes and the bond that, if you believe the poems, can only happen between mother's breast and baby. But no! The third verse begins: 'I crook the bottle.'

I read it over and over, thrilled, wondering how I've never read this poem before. I google Eavan Boland and discover she's lecturing at Stanford. I find her email and write her a gushing thank you for the poem. I don't write as a writer, it's as a mother: I tell her about the horrible birth and my attempts to breastfeed and my incessant pumping and feeding and the gratitude I feel to find a bottle-poem. Eavan responds the next day, she is grace and kindness itself. She describes bringing up her daughters in a more tolerant, less judgemental era and is gloriously kind about the awful pressure put on new mothers today. Her email puts a new pep in my formula-making.

Infant formula can be written and spoken about with a disdainful superiority but that disdained formula was life-giving for my baby. None of my cleaning co-workers judged me for not exclusively breastfeeding. I don't understand the tendency to dismiss different versions of parenting as wrong. I've read too many interviews in which celebrity mothers explain how having a positive attitude or doing breathing exercises or mantras was the reason they had a perfect natural birth and breastfed like a dream; it shuts out the rest of us who also did our best but came up against bad luck.

My daughter's palsy remedies itself with intensive multi-layered physio after thirteen months, but it gives me a small glimpse of what life is like for parents with children of more serious, longer-term additional needs. Not just the stress of dealing with the actual injury, but the need to explain why I'm clamping her lips shut as she feeds, why I'm feeding so frequently.

In a documentary about a fire station I once watched, a fireman said that they could be called to an emergency at any time so when they sat down to dinner on duty, he ate his dessert first. When I sit down to a meal, I eat my favourite thing first in case the baby's shrieks reach a pitch that takes my appetite and I need to pick her up.

The baby is fed many times a night and is awake anytime from 4.30 a.m. It's morning in her world, and so we get up. I get between three and five hours of sleep pieced together in half-hour lumps (her feeds have grown to thirty-minute intervals). It's always during these bouts I start thinking about the second novel: why amn't I writing it, will I ever write again? The early rise of the cleaning job meant my body was broken into sleeplessness years ago: it's used to snatch and grabs of sleep, but even still there are times when I don't know if I'm awake or asleep or how much time has passed. Some days I'm so tired I can't figure out traffic-light signals: it takes my brain a long time to process if I'm looking for red or green lights, red or green men, or to judge how near or far oncoming cars are. Those days I bring the baby across the road (one set of traffic lights to figure out) to a very small park. We trudge mindless laps over and over again, passing the same drug dealer on a bench waiting for his customers, on nodding terms now, neither a threat to the other's business.

My sister-in-law brings my one-year-old niece and their poodle to visit. My baby launches herself at the dog, trying to grab his tantalisingly fast-moving tail, but the dog nimbly sidesteps her. The baby then paws at her cousin's face, her cousin tries to kick her head. Meanwhile the poodle is trying to chew the baby's bottle and eat the one-year-old's mushy food. In a small house, it's hard to set three heedless creatures in orbit without antagonising each other, like the riddle of getting the fox and the goose and the bag of corn across the river intact and uneaten.

I have a daft tendency to believe what I read or hear over what I'm experiencing. If the weather forecast is for a dry evening, I find it hard to believe the actual raindrops that are wetting me. This adds to my aggrievement when I didn't get the naps I felt I was due, or the sleeping through the night I was promised at a certain stage. I'd imagined a maternity leave spent writing or baking during the two-hour naps I'd heard about, but there are no naps longer than thirty minutes until the baby is eight months old. I'd bought multiple silicone baking trays for cakes that were never baked, the trays remaining ungreased in the cupboard. I try to read in those thirty-minute time-pockets, one arm holding the gorgeous heft of her, one hand turning pages as silently as possible, but few sentences are read when there is a small mouth quivering and tiny eyelids flickering through baby-dreams to watch instead. When my partner comes home from work in the evening I tear upstairs to sleep for an uninterrupted couple of hours; those hours are my link to sanity these months. I often think about single parents of sleepless babies: just how?

At one point in the child's babyhood, I add up her night naps and day naps and calculate she's getting around half the recommended amount of sleep for a child her age. The doctor tells me she's absolutely fine, that children need different amounts of sleep, it's the parents who suffer the most. In one of my obsessive internet trawls for sleep solutions, I come across a study on Parents.com that found that when children don't get enough sleep, they can have a drop in IQ points equivalent to what's seen in a child who has lead poisoning: possibly the least helpful thing for a desperate parent to find.

The days become weeks, weeks become months. Several days a week I walk the baby into town in a sling on my chest. She is in raptures at new faces and places, flapping delightedly once we're moving and moving fast. If I take a bus or meet friends in cafés, she screams at the seatedness of it all so mostly I meet people for walks or visit museums with them or go to their houses where I can set her down to gnaw on somebody else's carpet. I bring the baby to the National Gallery. Every January the gallery displays its collection of J. M. W. Turner's watercolours, the conditions of the 1900 bequest being that the exhibition is free of charge and the paintings are shown in the month of lowest light. I love the altruism of the free-ness, and I love when practices are kept up long after the original reason for them has dropped away (low light can be artificially replicated nowadays). January had slipped by unheeded, and I make it to the gallery on the 31st. In the Turner room, I have only minutes for the quickest of glimpses of the paintings before the baby gets up a terrible wail. Back out to the main gallery and bright light: instant calm.

My parents mind the baby on Friday mornings so I can write. That's the plan. But her sleep is so fractured, my night-sleeps are more dozes and when my parents come I sleep. I've stopped dreaming, I can't get to the dream-stage.

I BRING THE BABY INTO TRINITY FOR A VISIT. MY supervisor brings me from kitchen to kitchen in the arts block, libraries and museum building to different cleaners I've worked with. The baby is passed around, thrilled with the new faces to look at; my co-workers dandle her and coo at her, giving gorgeous gifts, some hand-knitted. I'm told to get going on making the next baby, this one needs a sibling.

There are days when the only things keeping me going are coffee and sugary treats. I measure what kind of night the baby had by the teaspoons in the drawer: the number of clean teaspoons is inversely proportional to the amount of sleep my partner and I got, like Eliot's J. Alfred Prufrock: 'I have measured out my life with coffee spoons.' I think often of my grandmothers and the women I clean with, rearing larger families in an earlier era, who just got on with it. No prizes came their way for the dogged day-in-day-out-ness of it all.

I should be writing my novel. Or rejigging it into a workable structure. But if I can bring myself to open the laptop, I write fragments of this new life because I don't want to forget it, I am new to this ferocity of love. I can't stop holding her, kissing her, playing with her but it's a depth of feeling I can't find words for – or else it's been said so much better before. I'm mostly useless at keeping a diary but when I got laser eye surgery years ago I wrote about the difference, not wanting to forget the before. This is similar: I want to mark the change before it becomes normal. I take endless photos of her so I can remember what she looks like, I write about her so I can remember what she did, but I can't find a way to retain the physical sense of hugging her, holding her tiny body tight to my chest as if it's the rightest thing in the world.

I dip in and out of Tillie Olsen's book *Silences*, which explores why writers have periods of silence and blockage, with particular emphasis on women writers whose work or children hamper their productivity: 'How much it takes to become a writer. Bent (far more common than we assume), circumstances, time, development of craft – but beyond that: how much conviction as to the importance of what one has to say, one's right to say it.'

I leave the file of *Wunderland*, my novel-not-in-progress, guiltily unopened on my laptop. It feels so utterly irrelevant to be making up words about people who don't exist when what is happening in the real now-world is so much more momentous. But I also know that what is happening is only momentous to this baby's parents.

I'm struggling to go backwards into the novel so I attempt to go forwards into something new. I rummage through my notebooks and folders of paper scraps with writing ideas and come across *Choose Your Own Adventure* books, which I loved as a child. I've been rereading these books recently, ideal for a brain unable to focus on longer stories: read a short introduction then choose a direction, mostly ending up dead before choosing a different direction, staying alive and emerging heroic. They're very satisfying short bursts of adventure. I reach the planning stages of an essay about my love of *Choose Your Own Adventure* books, writing snippets and an introduction, and then I come across a *New Yorker* essay by Leslie Jamison on the topic. I get heart-sink, sulking for a while before copping myself on and enjoying it. Lots of writers probably loved those books as kids, our first experience of controlling the story.

My next idea is to write something about Japanese onomatopoeic words (similar to my obsession with German compound nouns that played out in my second novel). *Fuwa fuwa* = fluffy, *doki doki* = rapid heartbeat, *pakupaku* = eating food too quickly. I plan to structure a piece of writing around them but just as I'm trying to figure out what form I could write (an essay? Novel or nonfiction book based around relevant sounds?) I come across a beautiful book about Japanese onomatopoeia by Polly Barton, another writer I admire. There's surely a Japanese onomatopoeic word for being so particularly thwarted (*tooslow*, *tooslow*).

Then I start making a list of the towns between Dublin and Mayo we passed through on family trips to visit my father's homeplace, Belmullet, thinking of writing something structured by these placenames. But I find Paul Durcan's poem 'Going Home to Mayo', which also lists the towns he passes through with his father as a child. Maybe the universe is telling me to stop writing.

When she's five months old, the baby is diagnosed with hip dysplasia; the orthopaedic consultant mentions surgery. We're now in several different healthcare systems. I bring the baby to:

The public health nurse and doctor in the local health centre for weigh-ins.
A different GP for developmental checks.
The nurse in the GP practice for vaccinations.
The physio in the maternity hospital for neck and shoulder weakness from the birth injury, she lists to one side and needs help to correct her posture.
The dietitian in the maternity hospital for feeding issues from the palsy.
The paediatrician in the maternity hospital for the palsy.
Ophthalmology in the children's hospital for eye weakness from the palsy (there's talk of surgery here too).

The orthopaedic surgeon in the children's hospital for her hips.

Attending one healthcare professional and being asked what another said – trying to remember numbers (weight, degree of dysplasia, etc.) and exact medical diagnoses to report back is like an elaborate game of Chinese Whispers only with higher stakes. I feel a boiling anger at the fact she has to endure unnecessary pain and difficult treatments. We do the physio exercises several times a day: some days the child and I weep together through them. Why can't I just leave her alone to be a baby? If I have an hour or two without the baby, I should be writing. I try to write but instead I spend my time googling forceps, facial nerve palsy, tailbone injury. I'm an amateur expert on all of these but I'm none the wiser.

A facial palsy website describes forceps as 'large stainless steel salad servers', which sound more benign than my image of them as torture pincers from a robot lobster. Who could possibly think that a metal tongs on a newborn baby's soft head seemed like a good idea? And yet ... the thing that hurt her also saved her life.

A framed certificate in the paediatrics waiting room of the maternity hospital says it has been recognised as a baby-friendly environment. Like the warnings on packets of peanuts that say May Contain Traces of Nuts.

WHEN MY DAUGHTER IS EIGHT MONTHS OLD, I GO back to my cleaning job. After the six months of statutory maternity leave, I took two-and-a-half-months' unpaid leave to bring her up to a sturdier age when she's able to feed with no issues. I'm in horror at American mothers who are entitled to a grim zero weeks' paid maternity (and only guaranteed twelve weeks' unpaid leave) so many go back sooner.

On the first day of her crèche induction, I bring the baby in for half an hour and stay to help her settle in. She is agog at other babies, new toys. The second day, I bring her and leave her for half an hour. I sit in a café across the street sobbing into my cappuccino, wondering if I'm the worst mother in the world to abandon my baby. I quell the urge to run back to the crèche saying it was all a mistake, scoop her up in my arms and take her somewhere we could live with no childcare, no overpriced Dublin mortgage – in fact, who needs clothes and nappies, let's go full feral. I go back to the crèche thirty minutes later, ready to inform the manager of my new life plans when I see my daughter getting stuck into the toys, manhandling other babies, emitting delighted shrieks. She cries when I take her away and I know it's the right decision; we've reached a stage where I'm not enough for her.

The Luas tramline has been extended across the city and I can now get the first Luas at 5.30 a.m. into work, with thirty seconds' walk either side. This improves my life so radically that it's hard to remember having to walk in. I'm apprehensive about managing my cleaning job with lower-back pain, which, eight months after the birth, gives me no let-up. I'm afraid of having to give up a job I want to keep, need to keep, because of physical inability to do it but after a few weeks I realise that cleaning – even lugging heavy buckets and hoovering and bending and reaching – consists of controlled movements that are manageable. I can brace and bend at the knee and prepare for them. Easier than constantly bending and reaching and reacting to a baby, or twisting and lunging to grab her when she climbs up a bookshelf.

Going back to work is a shock to the system. I'm still up four or five times a night with a wakeful baby, sometimes for hours, but I have a ferocious appetite and determination to write, to get my brain in gear, to use this time to write. The baby goes to crèche three mornings a week and those mornings, I do my cleaning work until 9.30 a.m., then race home to do some hacking at *Wunderland* before picking her up at 1 p.m. Crèche, even part-time, is expensive so I have to justify paying for childcare by doing some real writing. I browbeat myself back into my manuscript. I print off the current draft, the better to take it all in as a paper entirety. It's daunting but also a relief to be doing the thing I've had low-grade dread about for months, it feels exciting to be stretching my brain back into writing shapes.

I'm constantly fighting the urge to sleep, and exist on caffeine. I get strep throat after a couple of weeks and need antibiotics. The GP tries to write a cert for time off work but I can't, I say, I'm only just back from maternity leave, I can't go out sick. A few weeks later, I have a pain in my stomach that steadily worsens. It's becoming hard to walk, I'm doubled over, and when my right leg gets sore and hard to lift, I google the symptoms: appendicitis. It's 11 p.m., our local A&E is hell at night, so I google *How long do I have until my appendix bursts?* The answer is 48–72 hours. I calculate that I have enough time to go to hospital first thing in the morning. I'd rather writhe in pain in bed than on a plastic chair watching the night antics of the Mater A&E. Next morning I go to hospital. This pain is half the intensity of labour pains (I rate it 5, nowhere near the 10+ of back labour in my pain scale). A CT scan shows appendicitis.

I'm kept topped up on a morphine drip before surgery. I'm treated like a sick patient, my descriptions of pain are listened to and acted on. After surgery, my opinions on pain (from a keyhole appendectomy) are taken far more seriously than the exponentially worse pain from botched childbirth, when I was fobbed off with paracetamol.

One of the cleaners I work with calls. Her first words are, 'You lucky bitch.' The work is hard when a burst appendix seems preferable. Some of the women on my ward are seriously ill. The woman who'd had all her insides taken out (as she put it) and would never leave the hospital, looks out the window and remarks, Great drying weather. She says, It's something you don't appreciate when you've to do it so often but I'd give anything to be hanging out clothes right now. I still think of her, years later, when I get to hang clean clothes on the washing line on a sunny day.

I'M GIVEN A MONTH OFF WORK, TOLD TO LIFT nothing heavier than a teacup. This is an unexpected windfall of writing time. I extend the baby's crèche days from three to five days a week and after I've recovered, I have a few weeks of exhaustion-free mornings to write and get properly stuck into the novel. I think I know where I'm going with it: this wad of time opens my mind up to various possibilities for structuring the book and sorting out the bockety timeline. The feeling lasts as long as my time off work. As soon as I'm back in work I'm shattered again. I'm up with the baby too many times before my 4.40 a.m. alarm beep. I soon lose momentum.

Tillie Olsen describes returning to paid work after a period of dedicated writing time, her writing failing this 'time of festering and congestion'. I love her definition of full-timeness – not actual hours spent writing but writing as your main profession, 'practised habitually, in freed, protected, undistracted time as needed, when it is needed'. Who has that?

In my quest for how writers manage it, I compulsively read How-I-Write or Why-I-Write books and articles, hoping for a glimpse at the secret.

Olsen describes Sylvia Plath getting up at 4 a.m. to write *Ariel* – the sheer effort that requires, to propel yourself to write before parenting duties begin, knowing you'll need so much energy for the children. (How absolutely revered Ted Hughes was, solely for his writing.) In Mason Currey's book *Daily Rituals*, I read about Frances Trollope who wrote to support her six children and sick husband; she started writing at 4 a.m. in order to have her writing done before getting breakfast ready. I'm in awe of Trollope and Plath, their persistence in getting up so early to write, work that doesn't have to be clocked into, forcing themselves to show up to.

Currey says Thomas Mann closed the door to his study at 9 a.m., 'making himself unavailable for visitors, telephone calls, or family. The children were strictly forbidden to make any noise between 9:00 and noon.' Never mind Thomas; how, Mrs Mann, how did you keep the children quiet for an entire morning? It's surely easier to write a book than to entertain children in silence for hours. Mark Twain apparently spent summers with his family at a farm, going into his study after breakfast six days a week and staying there till dinner at 5 p.m. His family 'would not venture near the study – they would blow a horn if they needed him – he could usually work uninterruptedly for several hours'. It seems desperately unfair to admire these men of genius and unlimited writing hours, and to ignore the women putting in the harder work unseen. I don't think I'll ever read Mann or Twain without thinking of their mean-spirited monofocus. But … maybe that's what it takes? To hell with the needs and wants of spouses and children, The Work is all that matters.

THERE ARE WHOLE PLOTLINES, NARRATIVE STRANDS, stories, paragraphs lost to my forgettings. I think up some phrase or idea while I'm walking or showering and, cocky as hell, I don't write it down because I just know I'll remember it. I don't remember it and I sit in front of the laptop trying to remember what it was I came up with. I sometimes return to the scene of this thought, trying to wheedle the memory back in a Proustian way, but it's gone. I imagine a book composed of all the sentences, phrases, ideas lost that will be somehow given back to me, maybe in a bound leather notebook on my deathbed.

Tillie Olsen, my new soothsayer, describes how the demands of family and work prevent 'an undistracted centre of being' – if you're not immediately available to write when it flows, it vanishes.

It's said of a particularly lazy cleaner in the college: it'd take three people to replace her; two dying and one dead.

Of another work-shy cleaner: she has two settings, slow and stop. Slow and Stop becomes her nickname, although not to her face (she's fairly hardy).

A worker who does very little work but constantly carries a bucket around as a prop is called B the Bucket.

Cleaning is only noticed when it's not done, its absence is commented on more than its presence, in the same way that mothers can be pounced on for their inadequacies, rarely praised for the daily above-and-beyond. (Hotel guests might blame the cleaner if they find a dirty sock or used condom under the bed, rather than hotel management for under-hiring and rush-working their cleaners.)

In the area I clean, my rota dictates that I hoover offices once a week, but if I obeyed the rota, the place would be filthy. (A warp: I've been reprimanded by a supervisor for emptying office bins every day when my rota says to empty them weekly – staff are supposed to use communal bins for food waste.)

Most of the tasks under the heading 'Exclusions' in my household manual, I've been asked to do – cleaning of walls, supply of tea-room equipment, washing cups, etc., cleaning inside and defrosting of refrigerators – until being told by other cleaners not to do them, don't be ruining it for the rest of us. This is a mindset that can seem lazy to people in salaried professions, but not going outside of your job boundaries is self-protection for the hourly-waged, as well as not putting a different worker out of a job if you veer into their territory. If I obey a request to wash windows, I'm putting the window-cleaner out of work.

There can be an expectation of us cleaners as a constant 24-hour presence with the combined skillset of a maintenance woman / painter / electrician / plumber / carpenter / window-cleaner / magician, a kind of super-janitor. I can only do what can be done in 3.5 hours in a 170-year-old building in need of updating. The skylights in an attic lecture room leak voraciously on rainy days. I position five buckets at various leak-points around the lecture room, but these are moved throughout the day and I come into work after rainy nights to puddles and pools. Grubby old pipes, walls and skirting boards will never scrub up well; the paint will chip and crumble and look worse than before. Old carpet stains cannot be removed, the warp of damp, bulging carpets will never flatten with my efforts, no amount of hoovering will add thread-count to a threadbare carpet. Chewing gum can be removed from desks with effort but there will be discoloured hack-marks. When I wash the old, untreated floorboards in my area, the wood looks pale and ugly; the only reason for cleaning is keeping germs at bay. Mine is an area that would look better uncleaned; I could make myself redundant.

In *A Manual for Cleaning Women*, Lucia Berlin's narrator alter ego, a cleaner of wealthy people's houses in America, gives advice to cleaners: 'Cleaning women: Let them know you are thorough. The first day put all the furniture back wrong ... five to ten inches off, or facing the wrong way ... Doing everything wrong not only reassures them you are thorough, it gives them a chance to be assertive and a "boss".'

When I first read this, I feel the bang of recognition: I too leave a fridge a little off kilter to show my thoroughness in cleaning behind it, especially if I know a supervisor will come checking. There was a supervisor once who could only be satisfied if she'd pulled you up on something, so I did things deliberately wrong in order to give her something to complain about. It was a finely balanced dance: the flaw had to be large enough to satisfy her in her scolding but small enough that she wouldn't come back checking up on you and bringing attention to your co-workers, the ultimate no-no, *Don't be bringing notice on us.*

Berlin also describes adding coins to the saucers of coins left by homeowners to test her honesty, then stealing things they didn't expect, like sleeping pills. I love the twistedness of that. When I worked as a carer in New York, the agency warned us that cash might be left lying around to test our honesty. A plate of coins on the hall table of one woman's apartment gave me the jitters even though it might just be an innocent plate of small odds; I took over from a night-shift carer, so how could the money test be reliable unless there were cameras in the apartment? In her book *Mrs. Woolf and the Servants*, Alison Light describes the nineteenth-century habit of mistresses testing servants by leaving coins around, and counting biscuits. A cleaner I know once took a sweet from a half-full box of sweets in an office she was cleaning. She was reprimanded by the owner of the box of sweets who had counted the sweets and knew one was missing. I'd like to survey everyone I know, a kind of Rorschach test of loyalties, and ask them: whose side are you on, the person who took the sweet or the person who complained?

My cubby contains a product called Zapit to dry out vomit so it can be cleaned up easier: the instructions read 'Sprinkle Zapit evenly on the mishap.' I like mishap, it covers many eventualities. I've cleaned rooms in Trinity that guests stayed in during the summer. Mondays after concerts and GAA matches were the worst for piss in the beds and vomit on the carpet. There was a soilage charge and a worker who wanted to earn extra cash could opt to clean up the excess soilage. It sometimes felt like a cat-and-mouse game with the leaky guest waiting until we were on a different floor to leg it from their room unseen.

THE LUAS STOP SEEMS TO HAVE BEEN BUILT IN A WIND tunnel – even in midsummer it feels cold at 5.30 a.m. I wear a long puffy coat to shield off the wind but it's hard to warm your body when you're fighting its rhythms. Whenever I have leave from work, I get fewer colds, bugs, doses. How nurses/midwives/doctors make important decisions with brains addled by shift changes boggles my mind. Passengers at our stop are hunched and huddled against cold and tiredness. Early mornings have their own specific micro-weather systems; dressing for pre-dawn means being overdressed later, two seasons in one day.

The smell of alcohol can be strong on the first Luas. Some have been drinking late into the night and drinking hard, or are pushing through on all-nighters. The slog of it, builders getting up after a feed of drink to work long, hard, physical hours. One morning, my neighbour carrying a hard hat stops, bends over and pukes, wipes his mouth and carries on to the Luas stop as if nothing has happened. The same early workers sit in the same places, get off at the same stops every morning. We stop for Broadstone at the plaza under construction, next to a large silo of Kilsaran Concrete. My half-awake brain recites the list of building materials advertised on the side of the silo: Plasters, Mortars, Renders, Screeds, a beautiful morning poetry. I google these materials many times to find out the difference between them, but this hour of the morning feels like a dream-state in which facts do not take root. Sometimes the Luas announcer goes on the fritz, telling us the next stop is Stephen's Green when it's Trinity. One morning she shouts PARNELL PARNELL PARNELL when we've gone a ways from Parnell. Most mornings, as we cross Abbey Street towards the quays, the announcer starts saying, 'Tram de—' and stops before she can say destination, as if she's been suddenly gagged or silenced.

One morning, after a particularly active night with the baby, I fall into a doze. I'm shaken awake by the construction worker beside me when the Luas hits Trinity, 'This is you?' I have enough time to rattle myself awake and off the tram before the door closes. Another morning, nearby passengers rush to help when my travel card gets stuck between the seat and the window, we just get it out in time.

Parts of parenthood are like opening an unwieldy jar: you try and try and try to get the baby to sleep with no success and then, just as she's reaching the stage of unbearable wakefulness, you pass her to another person who she instantly sleeps for.

In an office I clean there is a sink. On the draining board beside the sink is a blue-and-white striped jug holding cutlery, the old-fashioned kind my grandmother had. Every morning I hit the same kitchen at the same time and have the same memory of my granny making jelly in that jug on a Saturday evening. I can smell the sweet red jelly cubes and see the wood-handled carving knife she used to cut up the jelly and stir it. Decades later, in my own house, my partner watched me make jelly, wondering why I was using a carving knife to stir the jelly. I got that whoosh of reinterpreting things I thought were certainties – my granny used a knife because breaking up cubes was too much for her arthritic hands. She didn't then use a spoon to stir because she had already used the knife – and washing up involved filling a basin from the bathroom tap, so using as few implements as possible made more sense.

I love traditions followed unthinkingly, like the story of the young woman roasting a turkey for the first time and cutting off the ends before discovering her grandmother only did that because her oven was too small for a full turkey.

When I had a baby, I had no opinion one way or another about using a soother. If the baby wanted it, I'd give it to them, if they weren't bothered, I wouldn't. I believe that anything that makes babies happier without harming them is a good thing. It feels a bit like how I came at writing – sideways, with no preconceived notions or thoughts to career progression. I wrote a book because I wanted to write the story I wrote, I had a baby because I wanted to meet this child. I didn't set out to be a writer or mother, these noun-identities were incidental to the verb-action of writing or parenting.

Every three years, cleaners have to do a manual handling course. We shout up answers to the questions as a unit, some of the older hens skitting and laughing, not taking the instructor as seriously as he takes himself. The women are the rebels down the back, cackling at double entendres about the box we all have to take turns bending to lift and carry onto a table (Put some leg into it/It's all in the hips/Don't be putting your hands on me box). It's a reverse of builders catcalling a young female. When the instructor tells a story of a man injuring his back while hanging out the washing, there are roars of mocking laughter: Ah he overstretched himself the poor fella/First and last time he'll hang out the washing. The instructor isn't amused. The manual handling course I do when my sleepless daughter is ten months old is in a hot room after a busy morning's work. When the instructor's voice lapses into a particularly monotone lull, I fall asleep and am nudged awake by the cleaner and maintenance man on either side before I slip off the chair.

A clean, wrung-out cloth might just be the nicest thing. Like how a roast chicken is cooked when the juices run clear, I know a cloth is clean when the rinse-water runs clear.

Five months after going back to work, I'm expecting another baby. I'm deliriously happy and resign myself to another forty weeks of vomiting. Same cravings for sand, ice, hard-boiled eggs, sour oranges as the last pregnancy. Same retching at milky coffees and cream buns, my usual staple diet. After the previous botched birth, I'm apprehensive, knowing how suddenly and seriously things can go wrong. I take the physio's advice and pay for private maternity care this baby round, even though it seems flawed that medical recommendations to have a Caesarean section don't guarantee it, paying does. Private care means a consultant oversees the birth, buys you accountability. We have enough money, even if it'd be money better spent on the actual baby when it comes. The private clinic is like a parallel carpeted universe. I am listened to, heeded, there are discussions about my body and my decisions. There is no brisk just-get-on-with-it-Mum, this is all hand-holding, up-to-date glossy magazines, minuscule waiting times and I'm sorry for keeping you. When a midwife learns of my previous birth experience and says, That wouldn't have happened if you'd gone private, it's like a hammer blow to the stomach. How grim, how galling, how fucking wrong.

Moments like this I regret not following a career path in which talent and hard work is rewarded instead of writing, which involves a whole heap of luck and timing. If I didn't have a partner with a full-time job, and various grants for my writing, this life would not be possible. I frequently do the maths of (regular cleaning + sporadic writing earnings) minus (crèche fees + mortgage + bills). Since I've had my first book published, I've earned more from cleaning than from writing. The home economics don't add up.

We take the one-year-old for an orthopaedic appointment to check if her hip has righted itself. The consultant shows us the X-ray; the dysplasia is now in both hips, has worsened, and requires surgery next year. Damn, I thought she'd done her time with hospitals.

We go to Dollymount beach. My daughter scrabbles at the sand while we show her how to build sandcastles. My partner tells her to stop eating the sand, it'll make her belly sick. He looks to me for backup. I'm in the throes of scooping up sand and emptying it into my mouth, pregnancy cravings having their way. Yes, I say between crunches, no eating sand.

When I emerge from Trinity's Front Arch at 9.30 a.m., from quiet cobbles and grassy spaces into rush-hour bustle, I always feel a thrill, like I've been let out of school early. Watching people stride to work I'm grateful that my paid work is done, I won't be hemmed in by a desk and chair: the sheer freedom of this life. I can choose where to write and what to write and how to write it.

Accepted truisms that aren't true for me:

> Petrol station flowers are the worst.
> Every woman needs a crisp white shirt and an elegant, camel-coloured trench coat in her wardrobe (for what exactly?).
> There is bad wine at book launches (free wine, by my definition, can't be bad wine).

IF I HAVE EVERYTHING PREPARED: A SANDWICH made at 5 a.m., the kettle boiled a couple of minutes earlier while the one-year-old clings to my legs, the coffee granules in the cup, the laptop on the kitchen table but unopened (open invites key-smashing), a snack and drink for her, her cushion on the floor in front of the television, the remote in my hand, then I get exactly ten minutes while she eats her snack and is engrossed in nursery rhymes on YouTube. Any longer and she's wandering over to me to the laptop to 'help' me type. I can get a lot of food stuffed in my mouth and emails frenzied off in ten minutes. I hadn't looked on such a small pocket of time so intensely before, a scrap of time that can change the lay of the day if I've got through some pressing emails unimpeded.

I think of poet Adrienne Rich's comment that any time she's absorbed, her children are drawn to her, pulling her back: if the mother moves in spirit beyond her children they panic. I hear you, Adrienne. If I talk to somebody on the phone, my daughter divebombs me trying to hang up. If I open a book, it's grabbed from my hand and flung across the room. Her father is able to wander about distracted and unimpeded; my attention must be undiluted.

I'd like to write more with fewer interruptions but I also want to be interrupted if my child wants me, I'd rather defer my work than accomplish more. How my mind has shifted to accommodate a baby's needs is a hindrance to my writing: I can't see the bigger picture any more, I can't focus on the end of a project, I can't spiral ever inward to go deeper into my writing work, my mind is distracted by the very present tense, the immediate puddle the child wants to jump in (or lie in and drink). And yet, I want to be distracted, I want to play with her and cheer her puddle-slurping and push her on the swing. The advice I received from an older poet, whose kids are long reared, rings in my ears: the days are long but the years are short. I prioritise her over writing my novel because the novel will wait and being one year old won't.

My partner is so organised, he gets the breakfast dishes and spoons ready on the kitchen worktop the night before, sometimes the afternoon or morning before; he's so far ahead of himself he nearly meets himself the other way round. Like the Christmas lunch I have with the cleaners I worked with twenty years ago. December got too busy so we had it in January one year, then it moved to February, now it's

March or April and we don't know if it's Christmas past or Christmas future we're celebrating.

One morning I'm pushing my daughter on a swing in the playground and get chatting to the mother next to me. I mention putting the child watching nursery rhymes to buy me time to get the dinner started. She looks at me more with pity than judgement and says, 'We don't do screen-time in our family.' It's the first time I've heard the phrase 'screen-time' used in conversation, I hadn't known there was a term for how I was fucking up my child's life/future career/long-term happiness. How certain she is! I get a sudden burst of predictive schadenfreude: just you wait until your kid goes to a friend's house where TV is allowed, they won't budge from the screen for the entire playdate.

When my siblings and I were growing up in the 1980s, my parents decided not to give us toy guns; they figured there was enough real violence in the North on the news. But, my mother said, whenever we went to another child's house we would lunge for the toy guns, shooting at anything that moved: domestic gun control had backfired.

In the second-floor library I clean, I'm at eye level with the fancy top-floor rooms of a hotel on Pearse Street. Sometimes the occupants in white bathrobes open the curtains and step out onto their balconies for a smoke, a world away. A new building is under construction outside this window. I time my cleanings to watch the crane operator scale the steps inside the crane shaft at 7.30 a.m. (one set of stairs on one side, crossing to the other set on the other side). When he reaches his cab, he starts by opening and cleaning the windows of his miniature office in the sky. A sky-man on my early Luas tells me of the cold, how hard it is to stay warm so high in his crane cab. I want to ask how he manages the toileting situation but I'm not sure I want to hear the answer.

A writer friend advises me to keep receipts for writing-related expenses, books bought for a writing project, or a coffee meeting with a writer about a project. I could keep the receipt for the boat trip and books researching my Dublin Port piece for example but I don't because I don't fully understand what to do with these receipts. I got audited by Revenue when I first signed up for the artists' exemption in 2014. I started on the back foot, assuming the voicemails and emails claiming to be from Revenue were scams until someone finally got through to me and explained. I sent off years of tax documents, with handwritten notes explaining this and that. Revenue sent a cheque for a tax refund. After struggling through years of tax forms and endless calling of endlessly patient Revenue staff, I hire an accountant. He explains in a way I can understand, how keeping receipts works. There are grey-area earnings for things that might fit under the exemption, but I insist on being above board on every cent earned. I can't pass it off as moral honesty, more a stress of hiding money, however small, and being caught. I want to keep my tax record of the gobshite who pays too much.

I can't find a calculator the day I'm doing my taxes. I find it too fiddly to use the calculator on my laptop, flicking between files and tabs, and the touch-screen on my phone calculator is sensitive, adding zeroes where there are none. So I hit upon my daughter's Fisher Price toy cash register. It has large working numbers and an addition function and gives a very satisfying beep each time I press a button so there's no uncertainty as to whether I've entered it. My list of earnings is so short it can be fit on one page of a document, three-quarters of a page really. I find myself increasing the font size so I'm not embarrassed about how little space they take up. I show an accountant friend the cash register I've been using for calculations. He is dismayed, asks why I don't use a spreadsheet. Spreadsheets are complicated, I say, too complicated for such small numbers of small amounts of money. I send a photo of my calculating machine to my own accountant: silence. I am not impressing the accountants.

BEFORE I BECAME A CLEANER, I HADN'T REALISED how many conversations among a certain class of women revolve around hiring cleaners. Who's your cleaner/how much do you pay them/how good/fast are they/are they worth it? It rankles listening to otherwise decent people gleefully sharing tips on how to sneak in extra housework to the cleaner's tasks for no extra pay (leave a pile of ironing on the ironing board, see if she'll do it!) or keeping the kids awake for the babysitter to get your money's worth. There can be a discrepancy between someone with publicly virtuous credentials boast about getting the most out of low-waged female childminders and cleaners, a blind spot when it comes to The Help. Maybe it's easier to treat workers badly if you don't think they're from the same band of humanity as yourself. Or is it a self-protective thing, to look down on someone who knows the shape of your skid marks and the colour of your sheet stains?

Alison Light's book about Virginia Woolf's servants discusses the shortage of live-in servants in England after the First World War. She describes the 'eugenicist tinge' of these discussions, the implicit assumption that some women are built for slaving while others are built for leisure. Like the magazine articles today that advise their female readers: You're worth it! Take control of your life and hire a cleaner! but the women who do the cleaning are not worth it, they are only worth the hourly rate for their services. A woman whose office I clean tells me how busy and tired she is 'as a working mother'. Having witnessed me cleaning her office while pregnant, it doesn't seem to occur to her that I too might be a busy, tired working mother, my work doesn't have the same value.

I cleaned privately when I was a student, which I found harder than being part of a housekeeping team. One woman seemed to think I could transform her 1970s avocado bathroom with its decades of ingrained stains into a sparkling new bathroom and was disappointed by my failed efforts, grudgingly counting coins into my hand like a modern-day Scrooge. I also cleaned for a pleasant elderly couple who had decanted a family home's worth of stuff into a cramped apartment. They'd sit on the sofa watching me dust surfaces crammed with ornaments and lamps and random clutter. I grew clumsier under pressure, diving to rescue lamps and tchotchkes from falling, until eventually the woman asked me not to come back, that watching me lunge and grab at their possessions wasn't good for the man's weak heart.

I once answered an ad in a supermarket to clean a very large house. I should have been suspicious when the woman who answered the phone said she'd just hired someone, but she'd take my details just in case. Just in case turned out to be a couple of weeks later when she rang and said her previous cleaner had left her in the lurch. The first day, I did a three-hour stint. The woman asked if she could add my earnings onto next week's wages. I said I'd rather be paid then. She made it clear that finding the cash was a problem, but paid up in bad grace. There were issues of expectation: she thought that cleaning her teenagers' bedrooms would involve me picking up all the clothes from the floor, assessing them as clean or dirty, sorting them and tidying up their other stuff. I wasn't very assertive in my twenties but even I stopped short at doing a sniff test of strangers' smalls.

In the kitchen I washed up mounds of pots and pans, days' and dinner parties' worth of crockery with dried-in food crud. The woman said she had to rush out suddenly but she'd be back in time to pay me. She didn't come back. I wasn't experienced enough to know the scam, I naively finished my three hours, waited around and eventually left. When I rang her number repeatedly, there was no answer. When I called to the house for the money days later, there was no answer. There was no answer a week later when I called with my mother who paced angry laps of the perimeter like a caged bear seeking a means of entry, and I had to give up the three hours of wages as lost, knowing she'd probably already told the next cleaner that her previous cleaner left her in the lurch. I've since heard from other cleaners that this happened to them. Is this scam passed on at dinner parties in wealthy areas, how to screw over The Help?

Hiring cleaners and childminders is a job that seems to fall to women. I do my utmost to avoid the responsibility of being an employer but maybe outsourcing the hiring of childminders to a crèche is like being too cowardly to kill-boil shellfish but happily eating someone else's killings. When I read *Mrs. Woolf and the Servants*, I expected a snob and Virginia Woolf did seem to suffer her class's bigotry towards the working class, but she was also fundamentally a writer who just wanted to write, trapped in the role of managing servants. I was prepared for righteous indignation but felt sadness for her, despite the air of automatic superiority that she clearly had towards her servants. Women who are uncomfortable being served and cleaned for can come across as snooty. I've experienced very easy relationships with male academics and office staff, sometimes more so than with women whose offices I clean, because women can feel uneasy sitting while another woman empties their bin. When someone avoids eye contact or makes no chat, it can come from discomfort with the inequality of the arrangement, not necessarily snoot.

My older co-workers often have a very easy, bantery relationship with male lecturers, a kind of exasperated fondness somewhere between a wife and mother: would you look at the state of your room?

Common laments about The Help:

- 'I don't know why I pay the cleaner, I clean up before she comes anyway!' said with a mock-weary shake of the head. Homeowners need to clear away their stuff in order for the cleaner to clean the rooms, or else they need to pay the cleaner more to be a housekeeper too; we can't know which clothes are dirty and who they belong to.
- 'It's so hard to find good cleaners/childminders these days.' It might be easier to find good Help if The Help was paid decent wages.
- 'I'm too busy to clean.' The cleaners I work with get up at 3 or 4 a.m. to do their basic job, then either do overtime work in Trinity or go on to clean schools or offices or homes, or rush home to care for children or grandchildren or other dependants, or several of the above.

One morning in early secret pregnancy, I go to work and do my usual stealth-puking. It's not a crèche day so my partner brings in my one-year-old on his way to work at 9.30 as I finish. I take her to the park on the way home. She's antsy, can't settle on anything, hyper. We play for a few hours and after lunch I try to settle her for a nap so I can have one myself, but she's having none of it. Her brain is fixated on learning to walk, and being horizontal plays no part in her plans. I check my email and see one from the literary agent Jonathan Williams, asking for my phone number. When he calls, he says he has some good news: 'You've won the Rooney.' If he'd said 'prize' I might have understood, but all I can think of is, What's a Rooney? I ask him to repeat it and he explains that I've won the Rooney Prize for Irish Literature and he needs to check my date of birth, to make sure I'm under forty. I'll be thirty-nine and three-quarters at the prizegiving ceremony, just scraped in. The shock is unreal. My novel is out of print, my writing career completely stalled. There's a cheque for €10,000. There's overwhelming relief. This is my maternity health care and some childcare covered, all the care.

When my partner comes home, I'm so happy to tell him I've money to bring to the household. I often feel like a financial drain with my part-time job and virtually no writing income. Using savings not earnings to pay for crèche is not a long-term plan and this prize money will buy me some time. It also comes at the perfect time confidence-wise. I find it hard to keep momentum going with the second novel and have lost confidence in it. *Why bother* has seeped into my brain, a mantra that is hard to ignore. The mess surrounding my novel's publisher has made me lose courage. When you get no royalties, it makes you not want to sell any books. It changes your relationship to your written work, I don't want to talk about *Eggshells* or hear that someone has bought it, even though it's such a generous thing to buy someone's book and tell them what you like about it.

The prize ceremony is held in the provost's house in Trinity. I go through my dresses and find one that skims over the secret baby bump, I don't want to tell people yet. On the way into town, I get a phone call from the new babysitter who can't find our road. I spend the Luas journey talking her through where she is now and how to get to the house; there's no time to get nervous when something as fundamental as this is not sorted. It feels strange being in the provost's house as a guest; I cleaned it one summer almost twenty years ago as a student-helper. I love the house, the innocuous passage you go through to get there from the Front Square side, the grand saloon, the Downton Abbey-ish servants' staircase worn in the middle by busy footfalls, the small room off the kitchen that serves as the servants' quarters where we used to have our break. When I was first shown the entrance hall by the house cleaner two decades ago, she pointed out the celebrity names signed in the guest book. I took up the pen and made as if to sign, asking if I should put 'cleaner' or 'student' after my name. She snatched the pen off me with a wail of, Oh for the love of God put the pen down, that's not for the likes of us. I would have loved to add my name to the list of luminaries with the occupation 'housekeeping' after it.

I've invited family and friends, some are current or retired Trinity cleaners. They're giddy being in the gaffer's gaff, lashing into the wine and snacks, happy being served and spoiled. I love being able to invite people to something fancy without asking them to buy a book or pay an entrance fee. I'm still nervous making speeches and can't take a drink to calm my nerves, but I focus on acknowledging the cleaners who get up and do what they do without complaining, and with no public reward like this. A co-worker who cleans the provost's house has read his speech – it was left on his desk the day before – so I already know what he's going to say.

The next morning I get an email from an RTÉ producer asking me to do an interview on *The Ryan Tubridy Show*. I'm still clumsy at getting my point across; I know I should think like a politician and shoehorn in my three key ideas no matter what direction the interview takes, but I can end up listening passively and forgetting to speak. Tubridy asks how I'm going to spend the money. In my head I'm thinking obstetrician's fees so my next baby won't be butchered, but I say aloud the first item on the to-do list for the house, 'a water tank for the attic'. We agree that I'm living the dream.

I respond to a phone call requesting an interview with Canada's CBC in the playground with my daughter tearing around, grabbing her when she runs at a fast-moving swing, lunging for her when she jumps off a six-foot-high climbing platform. Luckily they'll schedule for later when my partner is home. I feature in the Barometer section of *The Irish Times*, alongside individuals who are having a good week (Tiger Woods) and a bad week (Bill Cosby). I end up as a clue in a Christmas crossword, a question on the UK TV quiz show *The Chase*: when an elderly relative happened across my cleaning job as a clue on the show one afternoon, she said she got such a shock she wasn't the better for it. I've never had so much exposure. I'm also asked to go on RTÉ's *Today* show, filmed in Cork for an eight-minute slot. The night before, I'm up a lot with a wakeful one-year-old which has made the morning sickness worse (exhaustion and stress exacerbate it). My co-workers know I'm going on TV, they don't know I'm pregnant. When I come into work looking grey, one of them rounds on me, You look awful washy, you can't go on TV like that. They'll put make-up on me, I say, I'm just tired. Don't let us down is the warning. After work, I take the train to Cork, trying to discreetly vomit into a bag while writing up interview responses for *The Washington Post* (*The Post*!). When I get to the studio, I have a ravenous post-puking hunger on me and eat the crisps and the biscuits in the green room, all of the crisps and the biscuits. I'm surrounded by a weather presenter and models for the fashion segment of the show who are built for TV with minuscule frames, none of whom go near the snacks so I gorge alone, a hog among gazelles.

It's my first time on TV. I can forget the cameras and the people watching at home if I just focus on the presenters, but my tendency to listen for the other person's news is not a useful one for live television. I don't take up enough space on the sofa. And I'm conscious of trying to hide my bump, it makes me awkward and wriggly. I don't watch myself back, or listen to myself back, ever. I would never be natural again if I saw what I was like naturally. When I get back to Dublin, a neighbour ambushes me. She was shocked to see me on the telly, she says, just shocked. She tells me how proud she was, she never thought that anyone from the road would end up on the telly 'for something good'. Then, as she leans closer to examine my face, she says that I looked very nice on the screen and why don't I look like that every day? It's the make-up, I say, they trowel it on. Well, she says patting my hand, you'll always have that.

I know that it's the cleaner part of the story that generates this additional media interest, but I have to remind myself that it's my writing that won me the prize when I hear the tail-end of a sneery remark. I get uncomfortable when my background is misinterpreted. I'm not a rags-to-riches story, there were no rags in my comfortable childhood. I have an English degree, I've had privileges and opportunities. I do need to work a job outside of writing and I don't have personal money but I have backup and a cushion surrounding me. (I'm downwardly mobile: my parents saved and made sacrifices for me and my siblings that I have mostly squandered on not following an ambitious career path.) I can't know real financial fears of hunger and homelessness.

My job choice can confound people, even when I explain that I'm happy doing it, well-meaning people often read their own dislike of cleaning into my experience and offer advice: why don't you teach creative writing/do some journalism/work in a library, usually followed by an example of a successful author who does just that.

As well as enjoying physical work, my hourly rate for my cleaning job is more than the hourly rate for the content-writing job I previously did, and because I work part-time, I pay less tax than I would in a full-time job. My permanent, pensionable job in the public sector has maternity pay and sick pay. I don't work a zero-hours contract on a minimum hourly rate with the fear arising from such job precarity. The interview I do for *The Washington Post* tries to explain this, that it's not as black and white as Cleaner Wins a Prize (a pun-loving friend amuses himself no end sending me Cleaner Sweeps the Board/Writer Cleans Up at Literary Prize Ceremony headlines). Cleaning wages in America are horrifically low and precarious, the jobs are incomparable.

When *The Washington Post* interview gains some traction online, I get lovely emails and letters from strangers in America and Mexico. An article in an Irish newspaper had described me as rearing my fourteen-month-old while working as a cleaner and writing, and this gave the impression that I'm parenting solo. When I get an email from a single mother in Mexico who works as a cleaner saying I'm inspiring, I feel like a fraud: her life is immeasurably harder than mine. The falsely linear narrative (rags to riches, cleaner to prize-winning author) implies that I can now ditch the smock because I've made it in the literary world. My life is not so clear-cut as that. (I may be guilty of partaking in this overly simplistic narrative: when I published *Eggshells* a few years ago I wrote about how my character came about after losing my job, the headline put on that piece is From Dole to Debut Novel, a heartwarming if false arc.) A prize of €10,000 is wonderful but it's not life-changing enough for me to give up work.

I'm invited to tell my story to a tech company. Usually, when literary festival organisers ask writers to participate in an event, they mention the speaking fee in that first email. (Writers at my level make so little from book sales we depend on these intermittent chunks of cash.) This email makes no mentions of money. I'm uncomfortable but I force myself to ask what the speaking fee is. It's suggested that I bring some books to sell. I agree but ask again what the speaking fee is. No matter that the date has been set, the thread runs instantly cold, the invitation goes no further. The irony of asking a cleaner to come and talk for free about my 'inspiring' story to people paid exponentially more than me, while I'm expected to be grateful for the roughly one euro profit I make per book I sell. The hours put into writing a talk, plus the hours I'm there, plus lugging a box of books there means that a couple of hours' cleaning overtime pays better.

Winning the Rooney Prize takes my first novel from out of print to a deal with a (reputable!) UK publisher, a second go of it three years after it came out in Ireland. I'm delighted, I thought the book had sunk indefinitely. It's a strange anticlimax of a publication – there's no launch or reviews because it has been launched and reviewed already. I'm invited to a glamorous-sounding publisher Christmas party in The Ivy in London but I'm too ill with pregnancy to attend. A sick bag isn't the smoothest conversation starter.

I meet a friend for breakfast after work one morning in a greasy spoon café at the markets where the fruit-workers go. It's no-nonsense, basic, perfect. I ask for tea and toast and am told to take a seat. The relief at not having to answer questions about colour/grain of bread, type of spreads, flavour of tea, size of cup, breed/fat content of milk, is immense. I sit at a table with my friend, shaky from sickness. The woman brings a metal hospital-teapot, a mug, and a plate with two thick slices of white batch toast spread with butter and halved. I love having so few decisions to make for such deliciousness. I love my local cafés where everyone is welcome and no one is judged, where portion sizes are indecently large, where they do half-portions of meat-two-types-of-potato-and-veg dinners for older people with a glass of milk. And doorstop-slabs of breakfast rolls that have builders, guards and prison officers queuing out the door.

Cleaners have our tipping points, something that galls us into rage or silent refusals. Mine is sweet wrappers. Worse at Christmas-time, Quality Street, Roses, miniature Hero wrappers lobbed in the general vicinity of the bin, which the lobber doesn't bother to pick up when they miss. I hoover the floor around the wrappers, empty the bin and leave the wrappers passive-aggressively alone. It's not the wrappers themselves that bother me, it's what it says about how the thrower views (or doesn't view) the cleaner. (Christmas for office staff is mince pie parties and drinks; for cleaners it's thanklessly busier than usual.)

The typical rubbish in the double lecture room used for group projects is eraser rubbings and pencil parings, cracked set squares and broken compasses, occasionally pieces of laminate wood snapped off from the sides of desks. I imagine my daughter having a tantrum and doing the same, relishing the cracking sound and the springing across the room. In November, though, the engineering students make large structures from cardboard and wood. Those mornings I dread climbing the stairs to the drawing office. There are dozens of large black bags of paper and cardboard waste, not to mention the huge amounts of cardboard and wood scattered over a vast floor space. It's physically impossible for one cleaner to do it. Other years it upset me – I used to feel pride in my work well done – but this year, a pregnant year, it's particularly bad. I take photos and make my first complaint. The students are asked to clean up after themselves or their grades will be affected. I can only imagine how well that went down. From now on, I go up to the lecture room, carry the usual amount of food rubbish down the two flights of stairs to the bins (four or five black bags) and leave the rest. I have to fight my instincts to leave the place rubbish-free and eventually the place gets cleaned by somebody who isn't me. There might be a lesson there.

A US FILM PRODUCTION COMPANY GETS IN TOUCH. They've seen the publicity surrounding the Rooney Prize and want to make *Eggshells* into a film. It feels strange: my book is the same book it was three years ago, but it's the exposure from the Rooney that brought it to the producers' attention. I sell the option to the US producers, and an Irish production company joins forces.

They send me a 27-page document about my intentions and the character's motivations and backstory; it reminds me of reading academic interpretations of *Eggshells*, which introduced themes and ideas I hadn't dreamed of. The producers want to know how I saw Vivian, and in truth, I didn't. I heard her voice, saw the world through her eyes, but I was situated inside Vivian's head and couldn't see her. I'm asked to put an age on her too, I had her vaguely somewhere between her twenties and forties but now specificity is required. This is my first inkling of how different screenwriting is. I answer questions on Vivian's religion, details of her childhood, significance of her dreams: things I'd never considered or if I had, I've forgotten. It's quite a magical experience reading such in-depth analysis of a character I invented and mostly consciously did not attribute motivation to, she took on a life of her own. A small part of me is whispering in glee: *I just made her up, should I tell them she's not real?*

Screenwriting is so circuitously collaborative, perhaps especially adapting a novel for the screen. We talk over and over into and out of ideas; it's hard to get used to after writing novels on my own. Every scene, every beat in every scene must have a point to it, driving the story forwards. It's precisely the opposite of how I write my novels, so steadfastly internal, and maybe, hopefully it will change my future writing into something that is more external, more pushy-forward, more readable, maybe even more commercial. *Wunderland* seems too far enmeshed in internals to rectify now. So far I've just written what interested me, following my own brain and writing what I myself would like to read, but that's a daftly non-strategic way to go about things. I've also never worked like this before; writing something to be given feedback on while it's a work in progress, I've only ever delivered a finished draft of a book before.

The crèche sends a link to an app to monitor my daughter's daily activities. I enter my passwords and when I get into the app, the first thing I see is customer ratings. My heart pounds for a half-second when I see a rating of 3.5 stars and wonder who in hell is rating my child and why does she only get 3.5 stars? Then I realise they're rating the site for ease of use. Steady on, Mama Bear.

Tiredness impacts my words, a poor thing for a writer. My nouns are the first to go. I lose the word iron and ask my partner has he seen the thing that flattens the clothes. A bill turns into the page with the amounts of money we owe on it. I lose the word surveyor and come up with contractor, I talk about a criminal in a high-profile case and his apprentice, meaning accomplice. I can see the shadow of the word, just out of reach, I can usually flail around successfully for a letter or two at the start or the end of the word, or a sounds like (trying to think of the phrase contact sport I know it's close to impact sport). It's like a flawed game of charades. Sometimes I try to persuade people my mistake was deliberate, and it makes more sense my way.

Exhausted, I swap words in a sentence. I say I'm going to make a coffee cup. Or half one word and half another, impromptu unintentional portmanteaus: I try to say summer is back at last/again to a neighbour after a load of rain, and say summer is back *aglast*. I imagine myself reaching on tiptoe to the top of a tree for a word, far beyond my reach. I sometimes substitute a nonsensical word for the one I need, or I stutter mutely, my lips moving, silence awkwardly growing while I search my memory banks for the right word, or any conceivably suitable word.

When I stop working for an unofficial break and sneak-boil a kettle for coffee, I set up a chemical buffer, spraying all around the outside of the room with cleaning fluid to distract from the coffee smell. I drink quickly, on stolen time. These mornings, when I walk heavy-footed and nauseously across Front Square, near the tunnel entrance to the provost's house, the Rooney Prize ceremony seems like a fever dream that might not have happened at all. I feel like Cinderella back to reality, my pumpkin carriage of a fancy night out swapped back for a mop and bucket.

I'm asked to contribute an essay about writing inspiration to an anthology. I'm wading through practicalities and physicalities, exhaustion and back pain and sickness and the here-and-now-ness of a small child. The essay is weighted down with it all, chippy and defensive. I'm quietly but thoroughly bitter about writers who become parents and somehow, *somehow*, don't let it impede their output, their quality, their careers. What I can't understand is not just the logistics of childcare – how to get the time to write – but how to get the brain-space to thoroughly lose myself in the work, especially coming towards the end of a book project where so much immersion is required to fully understand how it can all come together, how seemingly disparate things can connect. When I'm completely absorbed in a book or character's world, it opens up a magical serendipity, an almost drugged state of synchronicity in which everything seems connected, solutions to writing problems just appear fully formed, but I can't reach that state now.

There's a depth of thought I struggle to sustain, both in terms of quality and quantity. In her memoir *A Life's Work*, Rachel Cusk describes her first night out away from her new baby, the feeling of having been fitted with a taxi meter. That strikes me as the perfect analogy, the sense of being continually on the clock. If I'm away from my daughter, I get a physical lurch in my stomach and am constantly pulled back to the present: where is the child, when do I need to pick her up? My attention can never affix long on something else, I always feel I should be someplace else, a constant low-grade guilt like I've forgotten to feed a goldfish or there's food going off in the fridge. Not to mention the want: I want to be lying on the bed in a cuddle with her while she tries to yank out my eyebrows or reef out my hair. I want to hear her full-throated giggles and chortles as she tries to fling herself off the bed. Olsen's phrase that women are 'mediocre caretakers of their talent' stays with me: I don't prioritise writing. Some days, scrolling *The Guardian* or the *Daily Mail* showbiz news comes easier than writing.

Everything I write in these years is on the shorter end of the required word-count: if the brief is 2–3,000 words, my piece will come in at 2,000. I can't extend my thoughts, they don't run along the space they used to. When the anthology of writing inspiration is published, I flick through the other contributions and feel alienated from the poetic, theoretical essays about sources of inspiration, and put it in the attic.

My co-workers self-mockingly call ourselves bag ladies when we come in and out of work laden down with bags. We have bags because we bring milk in for the communal fridge, batteries to be recycled, a bag of bags for the grocery shopping on the way home to lug onto public transport; we return children's and grandchildren's clothes when they don't fit, bring presents in for various co-workers, all the detritus of life. We are bagged because there is a lot of baggage.

There are twenty keys on the bunch for my area. Some are unused, for locks since changed or doors long blocked up. One morning cleaners clock in to find a new, electronic, self-service key-collection system installed, replacing shouting numbers at weary security guards. Our bunches of keys have been tooled onto a tight metal coil that can't be manually opened, so defunct keys remain. The locksmith demonstrates how the small, unfeasibly phallic-shaped dongle is put into the safe, the pulling and pushing in the knack. A big backlog of cleaners gathers, trying to get going with this system, bantering about correct technique (you have to ram it in, no hanging about; it's all in the thrust!) sending the younger men ablush.

For the next few days there's confusion and delays at the safe while we figure out the new system, helping each other with codes and numbers, yanking and twiddling. There is muttering discontent: many of us had operated under a kind of unthinking muscle memory, our fingers working out the order of rooms in our areas by the arrangement of the keys on the ring; the smooth functioning of our work is disrupted. We have to unlearn and relearn, something we don't do a lot of in our jobs, part of the appeal is the routine. Like the discombobulation of a supermarket layout being changed, confounding the order of my shopping list, confusing my aisle-traipsing.

Happiness in my job is: when the security guard who's been on duty the night before hasn't locked all the lecture-room doors and the fire doors. Less foostering with cold stiff fingers.

I perform my *Sunday Miscellany* piece at the Project Arts Centre for the fiftieth anniversary celebrations of this radio essay programme. Fifty writers had each been given a year to write about, I'm to write about the year I was living in Japan. If I got the year of a relationship break-up or unemployment or worse, a dull year, would I have made something up? After a pukey morning unable to keep anything down, I say goodbye to my partner and child, get the Luas into town and am overcome with ravenous hunger, blood sugar starting to plummet before I've even hit town. Oh no, tear into Tesco, grab packets of Jelly Babies near the counter and manage to pay, feeling myself crashing quickly. I just about get the packet open, slide down the outside window of Tesco on Fleet Street and cram them into my mouth, thankful I got there before a full faint. Sitting pale and slumped on a cold footpath outside a supermarket gives me a glimpse of how people sitting outside shops asking for money are viewed, or not viewed.

When my blood sugar levels up, I get up and walk slowly to the theatre. I had been happy enough with what I'd written but now I panic. There's no ending to my essay, it just stops. (I've always had a problem finishing things. In secondary school, my English teacher scrawled at the bottom of an essay: You can't just STOP!) I scratch over my final words and sit outside the theatre, trying different endings. I'm nervous with public events anyway but low blood sugar adds a few jitters. I eat more jellies and try to see what my original ending was, under the scribbles, and write it out again. Part of my terror comes from fear of tripping. My centre of gravity is off kilter and I am lumbering awkward. And, to compound my nerves, I'm on after Kevin Barry, not just a writer but an unofficial comedian who has drawn a crowd of admirers. It goes fine, I don't fall or stumble, either my feet or my words. My parents and sister are in the audience: hearing my mother's unrestrained guffaw when I attempt humour is so reassuring. A highlight is introducing my dad to Kevin, two lads talking west of Ireland. I go for pizza with my family after, and a woman comes over to tell me she liked my piece. What a gorgeous thing to do, it makes me want to tell writers or any worker how much I appreciate their efforts.

My blood sugar has a tendency to crash in pregnancy. Mostly after I'd been puking and unable to eat again, sometimes at work. I take to carrying around chocolate or jelly babies for an instant sugar hit, but sometimes I'm caught short. One day I was walking through the Ilac Centre after a busy sick morning when the floor suddenly started rising up and I knew I had just seconds before I fainted. I stumbled into a café, grabbed a bottle of Coke from the fridge, and collapsed onto the seat to gulp it. The kindness of the girl working there, especially as my bump wasn't visible in a winter coat, who let me recover myself before paying. I also came a cropper outside an Aldi, crawling on the footpath, rooting through my shopping bags for the chocolate biscuits I'd bought, cramming them into my mouth. That day my blood sugar had been low unbeknownst to me, but when I unpacked the shopping bags after, they were full of sweets and biscuits and cakes, no normal food, my body ruling the shop.

I try to write *Wunderland*. I've left it for months now, writing is hard while sick. My focus veers towards immediate deadlines and talks. I give up again.

I work, for a time, alongside a cleaner who doesn't do bins. He chooses the office of a lecturer who's away on sabbatical to hide in and locks himself in, sleeping off the morning. The problem is, I share a floor with him, and the people whose offices he should be cleaning can't find him so they find me and complain about their bins not being emptied. I'm torn between not ratting out a co-worker and a need to defend myself. My non-sleeping co-workers are equally irate. The job has inbuilt capacity for breaks once the work gets done but it's felt that this lad is ripping the absolute piss, ruining it for the rest of us. When he eventually leaves (for a better-paid job elsewhere in the college), there is no collection for a present for him, no cake eaten on his last day, no bother gone to.

One morning, after a shaky start, I sit down in the small library in my area, trying to gather myself. A lecturer comes up the stairs, the creaks usually warn me to hop up with my cloth-prop, but I can't even rouse myself I feel so weak. She looks surprised to find me – cleaners are not supposed to be sitting in libraries they should be cleaning – but when I explain she offers to make me a cup of tea. The kindness of it, even if the thought of tea sends me retching again.

Another day I'm cleaning the office of a lecturer who never comes in early; I seldom see him during my working hours. I feel faint with puking and sit on his chair to gather myself. I hear him come up the stairs and force myself to get up. I spray some chemical onto a cloth and run it along his desk. He comes in and says good morning. I try and delay him with conversation so he doesn't sit down but he's busy and in no mood to chat. I move as slowly as I can through the office, talking all the while, hoping he has some things to do before he sits on his arse-warmed chair.

Lying with the sleepless child at night, thinking she's asleep and beginning the slow creep out the door but going too soon, the child bolts upright and calls *Mama*. Damn. Like opening the oven door before the cake is fully baked, it reverses progress.

IN JANUARY 2019 MY DAUGHTER GETS THE chickenpox. Her condition deteriorates into a serious bacterial infection, invasive Group A Strep (iGAS). She's in hospital for eleven nights, undergoing two surgeries. Her father and I take turns spending nights in a chair beside her bed, watching her. She's eighteen months old, so tiny to be so tubed. I can't write about it now, I alleviate my stress into notes but I can't cohere this thing into something meaningful, I can only live day to day, hospital to home, home to hospital. It's too much now, I'll write it later.

Soon after my daughter is released from hospital, I turn forty. My brother cooks a nice meal for the whole family and I have a thimbleful of bubbly wine. Alcohol makes me feel so queasy that I haven't had the inner conflict about whether to have the odd furtive drink while pregnant. We're still injecting IV antibiotics through a PICC line in the child's arm, but she's home. I spend the night of my fortieth rushing to the bathroom to puke, then looking in on the child in her cot, with a physical surge of gratitude. She's alive, she's well, we have her home.

The rubber gloves I wear for work are: blue for general areas, pink for toilet areas. The gloves I wear for deep-cleaning work at home are yellow Marigolds. I can't wear them without thinking of my grandmother's yellow and orange marigold flowers set in the front garden, a wind-ravaged garden savaged by gales from the Erris Atlantic, ducked low and sheltered by a wall. The sheer joy of the colour.

The cubby in my area is like a large shelved cupboard with no space to curl up and hide. In a previous area I worked, my cubby was the size of a small walk-in wardrobe. I made a makeshift seat on bales of toilet roll and one morning, I brought in tweezers and a mirror and sat under the low-hanging bulb, plucking my eyebrows. My supervisor suddenly opened the door and stared at me. I sheepishly put down the tweezers, picked up a cloth and cleaning spray, and got up. We both walked off in opposite directions, neither of us having spoken a word.

In the week before the first of every month, cleaners fill out housekeeping stores forms, Have you done your stores yet? We figure out what products we need to order: the usual bin bags and cloths, cleaning products, maybe a brush and dustpan (the tall, back-saving ones tend to go missing). We count the days in bin bags when stores are running low. In December we order for two months but it's hard to calculate rubbish in advance so we visit each other's areas to scrounge bags when we run out. There's a thinking that if you only order sparse stores it looks like you're doing very little work, so over-ordering is the norm. There are rumours (unfounded) of market stalls in Dublin selling the excess.

I like the Dutch architect Herman Hertzberger's description of the 'cupboardness of small children's play areas', the way kids use niches and nooks to hide stuff or creep into themselves. My daughter pulls chairs together and adds blankets, making forts and hideaways. When keys or money go missing from my bag, I search the corner behind the TV in the living room, the nest where this little magpie squirrels away her stolen treasures. I love hidey-holes and clear a shelf on the bookshelf and set tiny furniture in it for her to arrange her characters; I put an old printer's drawer upright in an alcove for shifting arrangements of miniature toys and characters. I've always loved miniatures, collecting mini sets of skittles from Christmas crackers, tiny dice smaller than a baby's fingernail, minuscule ceramic cups from various countries. World-building for someone not into gaming; small wonder I chose the Miniatur Wunderland for my novel setting.

I write a long nonfiction piece about my buffet breakfast obsession which I reckon I did a good job on but it's rejected from every single publication my agent submits to. I don't just feel disheartened, I feel foolish for wasting time and potential money earned.

The library I clean is filled with engineering books, magazines, and journals with titles like *Concrete*, reminding me of Daddy Pig's book *The Wonderful World of Concrete*, which, read as a bedtime story, sends Peppa Pig and her brother and mother off to sleep in jig time. The books are mostly technical ones, suited to experts and experts-in-training, but *An Engineer Imagines* by Peter Rice catches my eye, I'm drawn to the creative potential. I read a page or two a day, but it's too disjointed a way to read, with one ear open for my supervisor, so I buy my own copy.

A more suitable book for dipping into is the large hardback *Lighthouses of Ireland*. Each morning after I've cleaned the library, I take down the book and read about one lighthouse. When I spent holidays in my dad's corner of west Mayo, the bedroom of my uncle's house was swept by one, two, three white flashes from Eagle Island lighthouse. I was a poor sleeper and loved the company of the lighthouse, manned for much of my childhood; loved the idea of a keeper in a tube house on a small rock in the wild waves. It hits me that each lighthouse has its own specific code. Because Eagle Island had three flashes, I thought every lighthouse had three flashes. It's a childish way of thinking, an assumption that my experience is the same as that of others. (I used to think every man's chest was Frankensteined with crude stitch marks because my father had had major surgery as a child.)

I find some waste paper in the recycle bin and write out the codes of the lighthouse signal patterns, taking a lighthouse a day. There's no point to my doings, just a need to catalogue and keep the knowledge. I love old maps and atlases of places I may never go to and places that no longer exist; I love tide tables even though I rarely sea-swim. I had Vivian in *Eggshells* write names of street signs in her notebook as well as tracing maps of routes she walked: the urge to contain or make sense of the world. I was recently flicking through a cookery book of my mother's, thumbed and creased and crumbed and greased, scrawled with recipe tweaks and changes. On the inside of the back cover and on the page opposite, my father had written out the Morse code alphabet. It gave me a lurch: that's where I get my need to catalogue. Something about the painstaking pointlessness of the activity appealed to me, a curiosity for something with no ultimate aim.

Times when I'm washing piss from a bin or removing a condom from a lecture-room chair, I think of what a co-worker says to herself every morning when her alarm goes off at 3.30 a.m.: *there has to be a better way.*

I have a triangle of constant small bruises at the top of my thighs, a cleaning tattoo where the long desks in the

200-year-old lecture rooms hit. The space between the wooden benches and connected desks is so narrow I can only sidle sideways, crab-like, which is awkward in late pregnancy. You can see the rubbish from a few rows above or a few rows below, but not head on. I look from ground level at the front of the classroom, then count up rows and how far in until I come to it, crouch and either fumble around on my knees until I feel the apple core or empty coffee cup, or else I lean back and reach behind, scrabbling for the object that I can't see. At this angle I imagine myself like a stuck turtle, flailing and floundering, belly-bump high in the air. Hoovering underneath the benches requires the contortions of an acrobat.

My co-workers and I chat about putting up Christmas decorations: they describe cleaning the house top to bottom first, washing the windows, hoovering and dusting. I mention that I put up the decorations and the tree first and then hoover and clean, after all the pine needles and dust from atticked decorations have been dispersed. The women are horrified; they clean up afterwards too, but how do I live with myself knowing that under the Christmas tree is dirty and behind the window lights is grime? Very easily I think. I'm reminded of Eavan Boland's anecdote about teaching women who were new to poetry, and one woman saying she couldn't admit to writing poetry because her neighbours would think she doesn't wash her windows.

I'm not prone to overdoing needless work or causing myself unnecessary discomfort. I wear gardening knee-pads when I'm kneeling down to shine brasses or spring-clean, which sometimes causes a snigger of Who do you think you are? as if avoiding pain is a sign of thinking too highly of yourself: *notions*. I'm told of the heroism of certain cleaners, long since retired or dead, who insisted on scrubbing floors the old way, on their hands and knees with a scrubbing brush, and no knee-pads either. I'm told of cleaners who worked right up to the day they gave birth, as if this unthanked, unpaid-for heroism is something to aspire to.

Mornings we chat in our tiny kitchen over a cup of coffee, to warm us up before the work starts. When we hear the side door of the building open, we jump up and scatter in different directions, in case it's the supervisor. One morning I find myself up a staircase to a dead end in a different cleaner's area and have to come back down, caught rotten, like a kid on the gur. The camaraderie of it, some of us making it to our areas, the rest of us red-faced, covering over our dossing with prattling (if we don't stop talking, she can't tell us off).

A Mother's Day card is sent home from crèche in my daughter's bag. She has scrawled a blobby humanoid form on the outside, and inside is printed 'I love my mammy because ... [my daughter has dictated] ... she has new slippers.' I didn't have new slippers.

I stop working again this pregnancy at seven months: the baby is sitting so low that every few steps has me doubled over in pain. With the weeks I have left before giving birth, I make a plan and divide up my allotted hours. Staring down the baby barrel, I write in a frenzy. I finish an essay, I write a short story and make a plan for another story, and work at the novel. Later, I find that what I changed with the novel does not make sense, my brain was somewhere else.

I batch-cook and freeze meal portions (one of my constant unfulfilled intentions), defrost the freezer, sort newborn clothes from my first child; it's been such a short time since she wore those Babygros that I haven't had time to get nostalgic. A scan reveals the baby's head growing very large; the C-section is brought forward so a whole week of writing is now crammed into minutes of time. Even though I'm on a frenzied mission to finish the novel, it's a relief to have sit-down work after the manic painting phase of the previous pregnancy.

I submit a short story to a Yeats-themed anthology eight days before the baby is born. I'm never satisfied with any short stories I've written; it's too difficult a form for me. I've written my story about hermits for hire, the bearded old men hired by wealthy eighteenth-century English to live at the bottom of their garden dressed as druids. (When your work appears in an anthology, there is the added dread of standing out as the weakest link. A review later states that

Caitríona Lally's tale of the problems with a self-sufficient hermit-like existence was fun but a little insubstantial. Fair.)

In the days before the birth I research boys' names beginning with R (after the mostly unnamed character in my novel), which sends me to baby-naming websites with pastel blue colours and blurry photos of baby feet. I'm not thinking of baby names, I can't give a thought to naming a human I haven't met yet. (Both my children were unnamed for days until their faces met their names. My son was checked out of hospital at five days old, still nameless, Baby P.)

I do a CTRL + F search with the word 'fuck' in *Wunderland*. It appears sixty-six times.

It's surreal checking into hospital knowing the baby's date and day of birth in advance because this obstetrician operates on Tuesdays. The birth goes smoothly, neither party is damaged. There is another haemorrhage but a haemorrhage is a daintier thing in a C-section; it's hoovered up unseen. I vaguely notice a whispered tension in the theatre and then a lapsing drift in and out of consciousness.

I'm brought into the recovery ward; there are attempts to latch the baby to the breast. He's later diagnosed with a tongue-tie so latching is not possible. I assumed breastfeeding would happen easily this time, with a child that had undamaged facial nerves, but any disappointment I feel is immediately quelled by a midwife hurriedly asking if they can take my baby; a woman is being brought into the recovery ward who's critically ill. My partner is rushed out with the baby, an unconscious woman is stretchered into the cubicle opposite me. As she comes around, a midwife explains to her that she's lost her baby. She gets up a howl the likes of which I've never heard before, a sound from another world. I try not to sob, it's not my tragedy, but in my bloodless drift in and out of consciousness, I find myself trying to remember if I really had a baby or if I just dreamed him since he's nowhere to be seen. In later moments, when various midwives try to encourage the baby to latch onto the breast, it feels so insignificant, so privileged to obsess over feeding methods when I have a healthy baby. I also have Eavan Boland's reassurances in my ears. (That didn't stop me paying out €250 for a lactation consultant months later: she left half an hour early, 'forgot' to give me the €50 change I was owed until I reminded her, and 'accidentally' pocketed items from the table in the living room, which I had to ask for back.) This is to say that I'm capable of expansive feelings about the universe and my good fortune compared to the woman who lost her baby, but then something takes hold of me and I feel I should do what I'm being told I should be doing.

A doctor tells me I'm borderline for a transfusion. I hope fervently for one, I imagine I'll feel like a turbo-charged elite athlete after illicit blood-swapping but the consultant's decision is no, back to the iron tablets and sporadic anaemia. Again, after this birth, it's like a switch has been turned off in my body and the vomiting just stops. I can forget in a cruel instant what constant nausea and vomiting is like. This is why people's empathy is limited: if you're not currently cold/sore/sick, it's hard to imagine it.

I want to know what laundry detergent maternity hospitals use.

Things I thought I'd achieve on maternity leave:

Cakes baked.

Expertise on trees. My first child loved trees as a baby, her whole body going into spasms of joy when she lay flat in her pram and looked at the trees above. I tried to study trees, I decided she might like trees in childhood and I wanted to be able to teach her about them. I tend not to do things in moderation and bought nine books about trees. Eight-and-three-quarters of the books remain unread.

Studying Japanese. I had studied the language immediately after coming back from living in Japan; learning for the sake of it interested me more than practicality, and now I somehow believed seemed a good time to relearn it. The Japanese books remain unopened on the bookshelf.

Novel finished.

Things I did achieve on maternity leave:

Regained all the weight lost through pregnancy sickness and then some.

Things I seem to spend inordinate amounts of time doing:

Pulling small vest sleeves down from inside Babygros with a pincer finger-pair.

I fretted that because this baby's birth was so much easier, and his little body wasn't damaged, that my love for him wouldn't be so fierce. It is equally fierce, Mama Bear exponentialled.

MY PARTNER AND I GO TO A LOCAL CAFÉ FOR COFFEE when the baby is six days old. He has just been fed and is asleep. I lay him on the padded seat beside me. An older lady sits down beside him, smiles at him, frostier with me. He half-wakes as we're drinking our coffees and starts gnawing at his sleeve. The woman's expression turns to near-fury. That baby is hungry, she hisses at me, he's eating his cardigan. I don't have the will to explain he's always, always hungry, that we've been told not to feed him whenever he wants it because he's overfeeding and constantly vomiting, that we've been told to try to stretch him out between feeds. I also don't tell her I'm struggling with breastfeeding and don't really want to try to latch him on in public when it will likely end in failure, him screaming in hangry frustration and me trying to ignore the stares from other customers. I leave the rest of my coffee, pack him up again into his sling, quick as I can before I'm given out to for not wrapping him up warm enough or making him too warm and leave.

On the way home another elderly lady tells me how wonderful my partner is (for being beside me as I hold the baby). She tells me to get inside, that it's too cold for the child. It's 20 degrees. I don't seem to be moving fast enough so she changes tack to, It's too sunny, get him inside. She can't seem to make up her mind whether it's too hot or too cold, the main point is I have to get inside. The gall of me, daring to leave the house.

When I registered my first child's birth, I filled in 'Writer + Cleaner' under Mother's Occupation on the birth certificate. By the time the second child is born, twenty-one months later, my writing has clogged and stalled and I write 'Cleaner' in the same category. Later, when I fill in a census, Question 31 asks: Do you work as an employee or are you self-employed in your main job? My main job in terms of income is cleaning, I write 'Cleaner, Employee of Trinity College.' Nowhere is there space for my bitty jobbing life, nowhere is it noted on the census that I write books. I get a thrill of future erasure: in a century, my books will not exist, I will not have been a writer.

I read that Agatha Christie didn't consider herself a 'bona fide author' even after publishing ten books, and when filling out forms that asked for her occupation, she put 'married woman'. Mine is less of an imposter syndrome, more an identification with the job I spend most time at, that I earn more from.

On the way home from registering the baby, a couple sit opposite us on the Luas. They are antsy, agitated, like life has caught them in a bind. They immediately soften when they see the baby, cooing at him and telling us they have four young children who no longer live with them. The man says he loves the smell of babies' heads and asks if he can have a sniff. We say yes, and he leans over and inhales the boy's gorgeous milky smell, cups his downy head and kisses it. Before they get off at Broadstone, the woman leans forward and tells me urgently to enjoy these precious newborn days, that you can't get them back: her words have the bang of absolute truth about them.

The baby has a high temperature and is not feeding. This is very far from his personality so I take him to the GP. She sends us to hospital immediately, he's put on an IV drip of strong antibiotics. The word 'sepsis' is used and my brain switches off, *not this again*, but this has been caught, these strong antibiotics are preventative, I think. I don't want to freedom-of-information the hospital records and find out what exact stage it is. He is so small that in the hospital file his life is measured in days, twenty days old. We're brought to the neonatal ward, little pods all in a row with a corridor running down the outside like a train carriage. There's a fold-out bed for parents, which feels like the Sheraton after sleeping on a chair three months earlier when my daughter was in the same hospital. My phone recognises the hospital Wi-Fi, the noises from the machines are as familiar as a lullaby. I stay beside him at night, pumping milk. My partner does days.

It's a surreal, timeless time. I miss my daughter so much it's physical. I had reassured her, when I came home from the maternity hospital, that I wasn't going away again, and now I've disappeared. I ache for her physically, I ache for the sickly, tiny baby connected to tubes beside me, and when I ache I leak milk so I'm continually leaking, pumping, feeding. One night, when I go to heat up some formula in the ward kitchen, I pass the nurses' station, there's no one there. I see no other parents. It's so eerie I think of the book from the *Point Horror* series I loved as a teenager, set in a deserted hospital with a murderous staff member. The radio in the kitchen is playing Dario G's 'Sunchyme', a catchy nineties tune that I danced to in a student nightclub a couple of decades ago. It's a blast from a different, carefree world where the only thing on my mind would be whether to fake-smoke a cigarette to attract edgier lads. I'm three weeks post-birth but I lep around the room, dancing manically, ignoring the feeling that my insides are probably falling out and my boobs are going to explode. It feels good. In a film, a stern matron would appear and be horrified but nobody comes and I dance till the end of the tune, the bottle overheating and needing cooling.

Before I had children I had near-perfect health, but the time from having my first child in 2017 to early 2020 is full of medical visits, for me and the children. In all of these check-ups, diagnoses, treatment plans, pre-surgery chats, post-surgery chats, bedside doctor visits, I, a non-expert, am trying to process medical information while stressed or in pain or both. I do my best to listen and ask the relevant questions and then to relay that information to other necessary people, but I don't always get it right. My understanding is hampered by my mood or my illness or my dodgy hearing or my memory. I might focus on the tone of something one doctor will say or a throwaway comment a nurse might make; I might misremember their exact words, do them an injustice. I remember the very kind ones and the not-so-kind ones, not the in-between ones.

They are working long shifts under huge pressure in a system that is cruel on their time. In my job, I can say the wrong thing and do the wrong thing and I won't be formed into a narrative of an uncaring or incompetent doctor, I won't be hauled in front of an inquest to explain my decisions. I know if I freedom-of-informationed my medical records or my kids', there would be a different framing of what happened, a different emphasis, perhaps different facts. I may have missed whole medical things – for example, I didn't know I'd haemorrhaged during my first birth. I'd assumed every birth was an explosion of blood, assumed that everyone kept fainting after giving birth until a midwife giving me compression stockings and a vitamin K injection mentioned 'the type of birth you had': only then did I think to ask what kind of birth I'd had. Hospitals are so busy that if you don't ask the right questions of the right people at the right time, information can be missed, or the staff can assume a level of knowledge that isn't there. And how do you know to ask the relevant questions? Medics can't know what I don't know and can't be blamed for not explaining everything. And different manners and styles suit different patients. When I worked as a carer, some patients responded well to me. Others preferred my more bantery, extroverted colleagues.

When I started writing this book, I dredged up from memory my daughter's birth. I wrote it, then found a saved file on my laptop with the birth written shortly after the event, which differed in minor details. Is the version written immediately afterwards the most reliable one, or is the real one the story that has grown vaguer and less reliable about detail, but more fervent about feeling because while it's further from the facts, the feelings have taken years to build, accumulating angst? I hadn't remembered it was oxytocin to speed up contractions. Does it make my account more credible if I refer to something written soon afterwards? But how can my more immediate writings be considered reliable when I was the one in the thick of labour: can the patient be a reliable narrator when she's been awake for two nights, in deep pain and stressed?

I think of the poet Emily Cooper's words: 'I read somewhere that memories don't have a direct link to an event. A memory is never a memory of an actual thing, it's a memory of the last time you remembered that thing. It's a sequence, not a direct line.' I like the layeredness of it, the impossibility of trying to separate first memory from later ones.

My daughter sleeps better with white noise. A radio is turned to static in her room, but it tunes itself to random radio frequencies at night, sudden voices sinister on the monitor, small nocturnal hauntings.

Things that make me so happy in parenting:

> When the baby doesn't manage to put their *entire* hand in the dirty nappy during changing.

The things you do so often they become unthinkingly reflexive, things you know so physically you'd be hard-pressed to explain to someone else – like when I asked another cleaner the code for a locked room, she finger-punched the air and we guessed the code from the shape her fingers made – are as suddenly stopped as they were gradually learnt. Making infant formula with its one-scoop-to-30ml-of-water ratio, microwave-sterilising bottles with its 200ml-water-for-eight-minutes rule reminds me of working in a solicitor's office with piles of higgledy-piggledy, unalphabetised files on every surface and getting to know in which room and where exactly in which pile each file was: ultimately useless information as quickly lost as it was learnt. Knowing the kids' favourite characters, knowing useless things intimately: which bath toys squirt water from their beaks, which from their arse or trunk. What else could my brain be retaining if not that? My minutely specific knowledge is not valued. Remembering the elements of the periodic table and death tolls from wars is considered a sign of intelligence, but knowing the health history and food whims of children isn't.

There are days when I'm on maternity leave with the second child, when neither the first nor the second are sleeping, that hanging up my dressing gown feels like an achievement. I try to follow my practices from unemployment, like not going downstairs until I'm dressed. If I go downstairs at all, it's very hard to get myself and the baby back upstairs and I stay in my dressing gown longer than is good for my head. As this is my last child, I want to remember all of it. I can't stop looking at his excited little face in the pram and keep tripping up kerbs I'm so intently watching his expressions.

This maternity leave I go for shorter walks with the baby to reserve some energy for playing with the toddler. I walk him around the campus of Grangegorman, then when his eyes start to drop, I race the pram to a bench to read for the precise thirty minutes that he sleeps, just like his sister before him (is there some kind of timer wired into the genes?). I'm asked to contribute a short story to an anthology and my brain is so fried, I write the story about these days, these half-hour pockets of time. Exhaustion has depleted my imagination,

I can't invent something so I draw from reality and add a bit of wildness to it. It feels like a cop-out, writing reality in fiction form, but it's the best I can do. The short story is not my form and my own form is not good when I write it.

Recovery from this birth is much more straightforward. Like recovery from appendicitis or knee surgery, I follow a predictable post-surgery path, I keep inching better.

Sometimes an errand is all that's required to shape the day. I search for Brasso for weeks. Not with any great urgency, more, every time I go into a supermarket or Eurosaver or Dealz, I look for it. Nothing. I even google it, and find that a hardware on Capel Street stocks it. I manoeuvre the pram through the tight aisles but they're out of stock. It seems to take up the breadth of my maternity leave, this Brasso quest, even though I prefer the tarnished look of the doorknob and letterbox. When I go back to my cleaning job I bring home a bottle from my supplies, feeling a bit guilty and wondering if I should come clean. The full bottle has not been opened yet, our brasses still unpolished; it was the hunt for the thing, not the thing itself, that was the point.

Similarly, I spend months, even years, searching for the perfect bag. I have a magical belief that this bag will put an end to the forgetting of nappies or the inability to find wipes when they're needed, stop the rummage and root. I never find the bag.

Again, this maternity leave, I meet friends in town or they come to my house. I used to know Dublin by its cafés to write in, now I know the city by its cafés with sofas to lay a wriggly baby. Many of my friends don't have children: they bring news from the outside world, of jobs and exotic holidays and romance woes and joys.

Night-feeding the baby is like heating a bag of microwave popcorn: when the gaps between the pops get long enough you stop, when the gaps between the baby's sucks get long enough, you pull out the bottle. There is a sweet spot: stop the microwave too soon and you'll have lots of unpopped kernels, too late and you'll burn it. Stop the feeding too soon and you'll be up soon again to feed, too late and there'll be regurgitation and puking, a full change of nightclothes needed, comfort given.

Around five o'clock one morning, I wake to shouts and thuds and the sound of glass smashing outside. I get up to look out the window but the baby wakes so I tend to him, listening to the muffled noises that morph into a high-pitched squealing. It stops suddenly; after a while the bedroom lights up blue flashing. I look out and see our drug-dealer neighbour hobbling to an ambulance; at least he's vertical. A neighbour later tells me she was up early before work and saw what happened. Three lads got out of a taxi: two ran to the house and kicked in the door, dragging the debt-owing dealer out and beating him with a baseball bat. The third lad was tasked with calling the ambulance but he couldn't remember the address, stumbling down the street looking for a sign until he eventually found one before throwing away the burner phone. One job . . .

My partner and I take turns having a lie-in or taking the kids out on weekend mornings. One morning I meet a local woman on the way back from the playground. She tells me she saw my partner with the toddler the other day and said to herself, Isn't Caitríona so lucky, B is the best father. I mildly agree that he's a great father and wait for the compliment to be edged sideways to me. But no, she digs in; she jabs me in the arm and says severely, Do you know how lucky you are? She seems not to notice the two-month-old baby strapped to my chest, the almost-two-year-old in the buggy, the groceries packed into the bottom of the buggy, the rucksack full of groceries on my back, the three-litre drum of milk dangling from the fingers of one hand. (I couldn't have looked more martyred if I'd tried.) I'm very lucky, I say defeatedly, isn't he great. Sometimes it's not worth the fight: I will always fall below the bar, he will always be above.

I love when something I've done unwittingly for years becomes a thing. Health and wellness features start recommending *rucking*, fast walking with a loaded backpack as a way to get fit. They give tips on what to pack in your backpack. Are they not needlessly complicating things:

why not just walk to the shops and bring the shopping home on your back?

When I have the kids up, nappies changed, clean clothes on, hair brushed, breakfast eaten, kitchen cleaned up, all ready to leave the house, I feel a klaxon should be sounded to celebrate my victory.

I take part in a Rooney Prize panel of writers in Trinity. I've just returned from a weekend with my extended family: the kids slept even less in different cots in a strange house and I'm shattered. Practising basic hygiene is just about manageable before the event, forget frills. I do a reading from my book-to-be (it's strange reading from it not knowing if the book will ever be). It's a boiling hot night and my dress is stuck to me.

In the conversation afterwards, Carlo Gébler describes reading *Eggshells* with prisoners and how, after initial reluctance with her oddness and eccentricity, they responded well to my outsider character. I'm so touched and so tired I almost weep. Hearing this is worth more than anything, but I have no response. I don't know what to do with praise when it's handed to me on stage and I seem ungracious when I say nothing. I struggle to answer questions. When I'm this tired, I can only see blank space in my head where there used to be words. I can hear my words as if they're spoken by someone else, they make no sense.

That summer, when the baby is two months old, I give a couple of talks on writing to American creative-writing students. I try on dresses that don't fit – I'm between sizes and shapes, all bulge and ooze. I lost weight to pregnancy vomiting, but the gain back is joyous, newfound freedom in eating all around me. And pumping milk makes me ravenous, giving me more of an excuse to indulge. I find a dress that's at least dark to hide the belly, add a few layers under to mask any leaking milk, and put a dressing gown over it till I'm at the front door about to leave, to avoid spit-up and drool. Before my mother comes to mind the baby, I try to put on mascara but the baby senses that I'm leaving and screams. I give up with one eye done, forgetting to do the other eye when I arrive. (There are mothers who can withstand their babies wailing and carry on with the task at hand, I cannot.)

The students look so hopeful, taking notes and asking earnest questions. I feel like a fraud talking about writing to people who are writing while I am not. I have no core strength and am trying to stay balanced with no lectern to lean on, my shaking legs adding to the wobble. The first talk goes well, the students are engaged and enthusiastic. It makes my job much easier when I look out to faces that are listening or at least pretending to listen. (Recently, I found the talk on my laptop. It's uneven and disjointed, some points are started but never followed through, there's no coherent argument. It's only now I realise just how kind the audience was.)

For the second talk I have something similar prepared, but on the way in to deliver it I'm told this is a more casual event with fewer students; let's just sit around in a circle and chat about writing. I'm at the edge of my capabilities and can't suddenly ditch my talk to lead an interactive group activity I haven't prepared for.

When I taught English in primary schools in Japan, there would sometimes be a last-minute change of plan or a mistranslation of instructions resulting in me having to teach many more kids than expected or different age groups than I'd planned for. Teaching experience and back-up lesson plans got me through but today, in the fug of barely-holding-on exhaustion, there's no plan B and I run with a below-par plan A.

When I bring my son to his four-month developmental check-up, I get chatting to a couple with their four-month-old at the health centre. The mother says, Isn't it great when they sleep through the night? I look at her with pure hatred. I wouldn't know, I reply, attempting to ungrit my teeth. I tell her that neither my baby nor the toddler have ever slept through the night, that the baby wakes every couple of hours, the toddler more often, wanting to play, and that before she offers advice, no amount of sleep training or advice can force a child who is awake for hours to sleep. The mother looks sorry she ever initiated a conversation with this demented madwoman. I don't know what to do in these conversations. I don't want the other parent's pity or judgement or assumptions that if their child sleeps and mine doesn't, that I'm doing something wrong. I just want to slap them.

I read an article about getting your baby to sleep by a parenting 'expert'. It helpfully points out that 'most' babies sleep through the night by four months. My rage boils to a point in which I want to assemble a posse of babies outside his house and play their crying on loudspeaker all night long.

I don't envy people their money or possessions, their beauty or youth; but I have a visceral, spiteful envy of those whose children sleep. There is a week when the boy is four months and the girl has just turned two. She has gingivostomatitis, bleeding gums and painful mouth ulcers. There are three-hour stints of wakefulness and crying at night, followed by a half-hour or so of rest and then more screaming. The baby's two-hourly feeds are now a fond and distant memory; with a blocked nose and teething he's waking constantly, some kind of internal timer gone on the fritz. My partner has pulled a muscle in his back and is in agony on the couch, and anyway, my daughter has decided that only her mother can solve her current spate of problems. There are nights I'm almost delusional with tiredness, I sit on the floor in the bedroom beside her while she screeches hysterically and tries to pitch herself out of her cot, counting the minutes until the next Calpol dose. One night I don't even get to bed, I think I'm going mad. I call my mother when the morning hours get more reasonable, she comes over and babysits while I snatch some sleep. The sink of a weary head into a pillow: should be a word for the bliss of it.

When both kids are going through a particularly bad sleep phase, I dread going to bed, it's so much harder to get yourself up from sleeping to tend to them than from sitting. I go to bed later than I should, waiting on the 11.30 p.m. baby wake-up, which kickstarts the night.

Your sense of what constitutes a night's sleep changes in this lonely parallel universe; context is lost in the sleepless zone. A friend tells me he was on a wild night out and only got four hours' sleep. Instead of the expected sympathy, I ask with barely concealed envy, *Four consecutive hours?*

I know I'm tired when I find myself:

Falling asleep on my toast, an unintentional butter face mask (I Google and butter has no positive effects on the skin).

Googling Stannah stairlifts to make it up the stairs to bed.

Putting off the ironing for so long that the clothes are now out of season (like not answering emails, this is one of those tasks that if you leave long enough, becomes unnecessary). It's only when I see duvet covers in a homewares shop saying 'non-iron' that I realise some people actually iron their bedding.

Putting the rest of the clothes in the charity shop donations bag because it's just too much to iron them.
Letting mangoes, pineapples, melons rot on the kitchen counter because peeling and chopping fruit is just one task too many.
Falling asleep at the basin in the hairdresser's. Waking to my name repeated over and over, like coming around from an anaesthetic.
At the self-service tills in the supermarket, not only can I not find the barcodes in the items I'm buying, I keep forgetting what it is I'm looking for, turning the item over and over in my hands until my brain latches on.
Trying to sign for a package and realising I can't remember how to spell my own name. I casually turn the package over in my hands and copy it from that.

My two babies are so happy but so wakeful. The adage goes, you're only as happy as your unhappiest child. I'd stretch it to say, you're only as asleep as your wakiest child.

I have some wonderfully uneven phone friendships with various writers I don't get to see often because of distance or busyness. These friends send long voice-notes which I listen to as I cook or make up bottles. I reply with messages typed on my laptop. It's easier for me to see the thread of my news in writing than keep it in my head to speak it.

When the baby is five months old and his sister is two, I take them to the playground early in the morning. The baby naps in the buggy while I push the toddler on the swing. I love these mornings pushing my speed-loving daughter: there's something so meditative and soothing about the back-and-forth motion of a swing. Another toddler runs at us, I grab the swing to stop it (it's going fast) and smash my hand at an awkward angle on the bar. There's sudden pain and comic book stars in my eyes and a limp-hanging hand, oh no. The embarrassed mother grabs her kid, gathers her things and slinks off. I feel weak.

It's early, there's nobody else in the playground, I can't figure out what to do. I'm bobbing desultorily up and down on the see-saw with my daughter, the banjaxed hand resting on my lap, when a friend walks by with his dog. He trains football teams and knows basic injuries. I wave him over and tell him what happened. Squeeze my thumb, he says. I try but I can't connect my fingers. It's broken, he says. No it can't be, I say. But it is broken. At the hospital, the doctor says he hopes I don't play piano, it's a complicated fracture, the hand will never fully recover. I tell any doctor or nurse who'll listen that I have a small baby, please, how do I do this, I need my right hand. As the nurse is applying the plaster of Paris, we're talking quietly in the cubicle about managing the baby stuff one-handed. She pulls back the curtain and walks over to the communal area to get more plaster, shouting back, 'Just make sure to wipe the poo with your other hand' to a ward full of people who don't know it's baby poo she's talking about.

Pushing the double buggy with my weaker left hand is hard, as is changing the baby's nappies while he kicks and lashes and arches and writhes (the toddler's are more doable one-handed, she can be bribed with milk to stay still). Lifting the kids one-handed is manageable, but each have been bopped on the head by a hard cast used for leverage. I can feed the baby and roll him awkwardly into the cot with one hand. I can't unbutton so I retire my jeans for tracksuits. One day I go into town with the baby in the pram. I walk around the Ilac Centre in a tracksuit, proud that I can manage a town trip with a broken hand and a baby. I notice some better-dressed people giving me disgusted looks and I realise they see me as someone who was injured in a more violent way. Oof.

I attend the fracture clinic several times to get the hand X-rayed and another cast put on. My injury is, according to the doctor, consistent with a punch injury; most of the other broken-handers are hardy-looking lads in their twenties and thirties. On the waiting room TV, cleaning ads recur with obnoxious frequency. A woman in one ad grins manically while holding a tub of an apparently magic laundry potion. She is wearing an open button-down shirt with a white T-shirt underneath. The image is suitably sexless and highly efficient. For some reason, Busy Mum is often shown wearing the kind of shirt worn by people in boardroom meetings, creased to perfection. This is madness to me. Who has the time or the inclination to iron a shirt for doing the housework? Why not show mothers wearing hoodies that aren't fussed by creases and T-shirts in colours that mask food spills and body emissions?

In films and on TV, Busy Mum gathers up piles of clothes from her children's bedroom floors and puts them all in the wash basket or the washing machine. What a colossal waste of effort! I do the sniff test in combination with the visible stain test: any item of children's clothing that can be made presentable with a quick wipe of a wet J-cloth avoids the washing machine and gets another wear out of it. I'd like to claim that this is for environmental reasons.

I write some stuff on the laptop about having a broken hand. Lots of letters are missing, I'm typing one-handed with the wrong hand and trying to keep up with my brain. I procrastinate nicely from the novel-writing with writing-adjacent activities. I google upcoming writing competitions and imagine turning my hand to a new form, poetry or flash fiction – plenty of writers seem to straddle genres seamlessly, maybe I could too. I spend time writing closing dates of these competitions in my diary and making notes on something I barely start never mind finish, let alone get round to sending.

I try to read myself back into my novel; I feel a bit fraudulent calling it a work in progress because progress has stalled so dramatically. I find mistakes, so many logistical mistakes that will take time to fix and I don't have the energy to figure out how. When you stall at a writing project, it matters where the project is when you stall. If I had the novel clear in my head, where the characters were going, it would be easier to get back in, but I'm stuck. I've gone the wrong way entirely. When I wrote my first draft, I had felt a compulsion to use all the notes I made in my three visits to the Miniatur Wunderland so there are long descriptions of things but very little happening. If you're not obsessed with miniatures this is a hellishly boring book, but I don't know what the book is if it isn't Wunderland descriptions.

The novel's timeline is completely off; there are days and nights that overlap or where time goes backwards. I'd intended to have my two characters narrate the time they spend together, sometimes overlapping, telling the same story but from different perspectives, and sometimes propelling the story forward individually. A fine idea but with years of different drafts and attempts to fix it, there are layers of time, whole new concepts of time in which the three original days have now sprouted more hours, days now consist of several consecutive mornings or nights without end. The male character's split shifts in his cleaning job have further bewildered the timeline. It's impossible to correct such chronology with a mithered brain, in a snatched hour here and there. The novel's wonky chronology feels in some way connected to my own bockety body clock in which day has become night; it's hard to fix the book's timeline without sorting out my own first. And, working piecemeal is less efficient than getting a run at it, coming at it sporadically leaves continuity problems. Also, my thinking has changed in the interim years. My female character is 42, but writing as a 35-year-old I gave her dodgy knees and hips and added in a decrepit middle age that my indignant 40-year-old writer self tones down. I started with Wayne Rooney as an England goal-scorer and updated it to Harry Kane after Rooney ages out of goaling. More fundamentally, I become uncomfortable with the very premise of the book.

My initial idea had been to write about a false accusation, the germ of which was inspired by an incident in my cleaning job. Shortly after I began, a man working in the building I was cleaning asked if I'd seen a coffee-maker that had gone missing from a kitchen. I told him I hadn't even noticed it missing. He wasn't happy. Over the next day or two, momentum gathered. A woman who worked in the building asked me if I knew where it was. She made it clear she suspected me. I suggested someone from another office might have borrowed it. She said the guards had been called, which was laughable, but she seemed serious. The man came back and talked about a mole within us, but they'd get to the bottom of this. Despite the ludicrousness of the Poirot-Miss Marple double act, I got nervous. My supervisor didn't know me well enough yet to trust I hadn't robbed a coffee-maker, because for whatever reason these people needed to believe that I had. A day or so later I went hunting in another cleaner's area and found it in a kitchen there. I brought it back up to the original kitchen and told the man, but the fact that the person they suspected of thieving had found it seemed too convenient and cemented their beliefs that I was involved. It made me see how vulnerable the low-waged are, how quickly the cleaner gets scapegoated.

Around this time I was inventing the backstory of my character Roy (who R has finally become) and this feeling of a false accusation was in my head. I increased the scale of the wrong he was accused of to raise the stakes in the novel – getting too close to a child – and left his intentions and the actual details ambiguous. It was the kernel on which *Wunderland* had begun in my head, a reason someone would leave a country under accusation. It needed to be serious enough that he'd leave home and for it to fester in his head and affect his dealings with the world. But I felt a strain writing something like that, when the more real and prevalent and vicious crimes in reality were kids being groomed or abused who either couldn't make their voices heard or weren't believed when they did. That sat very wrong with me but I was too entrenched to do anything about it, way too attached to my original plot. Something that started emotionally, a reaction to the upset of being suspected of something very minor, had expanded into something too big for me. This is the kind of theme that could be played out in a short story that I could have shelved if it didn't sit right. In the thick of very-small-child-rearing, this topic was too much for me, but now, with a bit of distance and more sleep, I'd find it easier to write. For all the novel's flaws, I can see its merits, its oblique angles and oddities. Looking back I can appreciate how hard-got this book was, with its ambitious narration and difficult themes.

ONE LUNCHTIME I GO TO THE PUB WITH THE BABY, a cosy local where I meet friends for the odd afternoon pint or evening session. It's a Dublin GAA pub with a clientele sympathetic to this Mayo supporter – when I came in one evening with a friend in my Mayo jersey after yet another All-Ireland loss, there was decency behind the teasing and commiserative pints were forthcoming. There are sofas I can lay the baby on to sleep if I time it with his half-hour nap. I can eat a toasted cheese sandwich and drink a pint of cider and feel normal. I figure I can just about manage with the broken hand. When I walk in the door, the pub owner sees me and asks what happened. Playground injury, I say. And what does the other mother look like, he asks. I love Dublin wit even if I'm not quick enough to come back with a response. I sit with my toastie, cut up for me by the owner while the child naps, builders come in off a nearby site for their lunch and a half-pint, chuck the baby under the chin, I feel human, part of the world.

When I'm pushing the double buggy one-handed, in supermarkets when I'm weaving with a basket or backing up a step or steep kerb, kindly people often ask, Can you manage? What a lovely phrase.

I see a recipe for vegetable muffins online. Why would you take some things that taste just fine on their own and mix them with something delicious to produce something disgusting? I'm sticking with my accidental discovery of how to get more vegetables into my kids. I start eating chopped-up carrots or cucumber then drop some, they lunge for them. The sense of scarcity (Mammy's eating all the vegetables) combined with the thrill of eating dirty floor-food.

There are many months in which the only writing I do is starting unfinished notebooks of medical issues or feeding schedules for medical professionals. Either side of the age of two my daughter is the most manic, she comes at me when she sees me occupied with phone or laptop and the message goes into the drafts folder. The only time I can send a text is if I distract her with milk and TV and cower down behind the kitchen counters, or stand with my arms above my head texting while she lunges at my legs.

I do an ill-advised search for my name on Twitter. 'Robin' has posted a review of my first novel. I follow the link to Goodreads:

*** spoiler alert ** No plot. Pointless ending. Weird woman. *Possible spoilers for this utter non-story*.*

I consider using her words as an alternative title of any reprint, *This Utter Non-Story*.

Robin gives me two stars, which seems a bit generous; the rating doesn't match her words. Unlike Alison, whose comments at least match her rating: one star and a one-word review:

Nope.

I google Alison, wondering what makes her so definite in her views, and discover she's an associate professor in women's literature.

At some point, my partner discovers that singing 'Silent Night' is the only way to get first my daughter, then my son to sleep. For more than a year, I sing the same verse of 'Silent Night' on repeat. I change 'Round yon Virgin' to 'Round yon purple' because I don't want to have to answer questions about virgins. I sing it so many times each night that I sometimes wonder if my voice is still going, if the words are still coming out, I've moved to a place beyond the song. On noisy firework nights (New Year's Eve, Halloween) when the local lads are setting them off under the bridge beside us and the bangs rattle the house like bombs, I cover my son's ears and sing 'Silent Night' for as long as it takes the fireworks to stop. On Christmas Eve when the local lads on scrambler motorbikes race each other up and down the road through the night, a cacophony of revving and roaring, I sing it to him. Like a stopped clock is right twice a day, 'Silent Night' is finally timely.

Some days my parenting style could best be described as cowering in a corner of the kitchen cramming Lidl knock-off chocolate mini-rolls into my mouth. When new parents ask me for advice, I'll tell them to unwrap the mini-rolls when you buy them, or the wrapper will give you away. And choose your secret snack carefully – a crunchy biscuit would alert little ears. I stash my chocolate in the sink while the kids are too small to see in. I'm turned away, Mammy's working, and yes I am, I'm working at getting the chocolate as fast as possible into my maw. I wear hoodies with pouches and tracksuit bottoms with pockets, the better to hide chocolate in. I also use a tea towel to transport chocolate to where I need it; like my cloth + spray prop in my cleaning job, the kids leave me alone if they think I'm working. I'm almost caught rotten one day when I've put the kids on cushions in front of the television with their healthy snack while I munch on chocolate on the sofa behind them. They come to me with a book about building sites. As I read aloud, the kids start sniffing the air, my daughter starts scratching the book and sniffing it, I smell chocolate, Mammy, it must be a scratch-and-sniff book. Must be.

If my children carry one piece of wisdom from me through their lives, I would like it to be the concept of breakfast dessert.

Time has simultaneously slowed down and sped up since having children, from the two-and-a-half days in labour with my first child when day and night lost all meaning. The days can seem extremely long with new babies and I can't imagine them not lasting forever. When my first child was born I found myself saving nice Babygros for 'good wear' that never came, not realising she'd grow out of them in weeks. I spent months puzzling over storage solutions for clothes or nappies or muslins, then not needing the storage before figuring out a solution. The time-suck: misreading time, forgetting it's temporary because it's so intense, like illness.

Especially for the second child, time seems fraught with importance, the pressure to appreciate him and his babyhood as he's my last. Time gains a new meaning when they start talking: everything past tense to them is yesterday, everything future is tomorrow: I like the immediacy, it nullifies the adult preoccupation with future-planning or past-mulling.

Some nights I build towers of colourful foam blocks on the sitting-room floor. When they get up in the morning, the kids can indulge in some instant destruction: their own personal Carthage to raze to the ground.

I'm doing an online talk for the Irish embassy in Mexico; there's a test call a few days before. My partner is downstairs with the children, we've pretended Mammy has gone out or they won't leave me in peace. I put the laptop on some cushions in the back bedroom, I forgot to bring in a chair to perch it on. It's so low, I have to kneel on my hunkers to get my face on camera. I've no time to fix up the room or my appearance or do a preview to figure out where my face will be. I join the call to see several faces, including a member of the tech team explaining how the actual event will go. I realise the Wi-Fi is weak in the back of the house, but if I move to a room with a stronger signal, the kids will hear my footsteps and come running. The tech person is explaining how important it is to have a plain, professional-looking background, I see my son's cot behind me, pyjamas hanging over the edge, toys everywhere. I grimace.

There's a sudden crash in the kitchen below and almighty screams start up from my daughter: she has fallen off a chair and smacked her head off the floor tiles. I'm in agony, I have a physical pull to run down and see if she's okay, comfort her; all I can hear are wails of *Maaaaaammyyyyy*. I see my face pinched and agonised on-screen, looking to the side towards her screams. The Wi-Fi drops, the screen freezes, and when I get back on the call, the tech guy is speaking Spanish. Either the other Irish participants speak Spanish or aren't fazed by this. Should I say I don't understand? As always, my face gives me away and the IT guy explains that the bit I'd missed when the Wi-Fi froze was something about a button automatically translating, but I can't find this button on my laptop or else I don't have it. I feel like the slowest person holding up everyone in a class. The tech guy returns to speaking English. I've now been squashed on my hunkers on the floor for too long and I get a calf cramp so my face mostly disappears off-screen while I stretch out my leg, bashing it on the floor to ease the muscle out, *Bang bang bang*. My daughter is still shrieking downstairs – I have to work to convince the tech guy that I will be in a different, more professional location for the actual event, I will be a different, more professional person (a non-mother) with a better computer and stronger Wi-Fi, there will be no cot or pyjamas in the background, no children crying, no desperately divided mother.

I write my talk for this event, finding it hard to pitch. I'm in a writing funk so the talk is of failure to complete my second novel. If I had to give the talk on a prize-winning day or publishing-offer day, or even a productive-writing day, the content would be different. (A friend trying to decide whether to have a child saw me sprinting home with the kids one rainy day, pushing the buggy with one hand, both kids screaming and pushing off the rain cover while I leaned over to push it back down. My friend saw the sheer inelegance of the situation and told me it was a factor in deciding not to have children.)

I do the actual event in a friend's university office: no baby's cot, only history books in the background, making me look more professional than I am. It's hard to gauge how well a talk goes online with no audience feedback. I'm never sure with these things if I've correctly unmuted myself or if there's a sound issue I'm unaware of because I'm following my handwritten notes to the letter and not looking at the screen for comments. My talk is being simultaneously translated into Spanish. When I mistakenly say the wrong word or leave a gap when I can't think of the right word, I wonder if the interpreter translates my incorrect word into the correct Spanish word or if she translates directly, does she give the word she thinks I'm looking for when I draw blank? I hope she gets paid extra for her efforts.

When I was seventeen I kept two fake dates of birth in my head: an underage one so I could get child bus fares and an overage one so I could get served in pubs. I'm reminded of this when I chat casually with some parents who hold themselves to higher standards, hiding the not-from-scratch and highly processed snacks I feed my kids and how much TV I let them watch.

I find the day-in-day-out-ness of cooking a chore. Some people claim to find cooking relaxing, I find it relaxing in the same way that a root canal is relaxing. I try to cook meals in one pot: stews, soups, pies. I like directing all my efforts singly, having to only remember not to burn one thing. There's a moment of satisfaction, after all the measuring and chopping, when I put the contents in the saucepan and set it to boil: that perfect moment when it's right so far and could feasibly keep going right. I used to do stuffed chicken thighs in the oven, thinking that the 22-minute cooking time was a strange number to land on, but following the timing exactly. Then one day I realised I had only read half the instructions. The entire guidelines were: cook for twenty-two minutes in the oven, turn, and then cook for a further twenty-three minutes. Oops.

When I look for something new to cook, I google 'simple recipe for … quick recipe for …' My partner googles 'one-pot'. If I don't know two of the ingredients I skip it. When I see recipes that use 'store cupboard essentials' I can be fairly certain it's not my store cupboard they're talking about.

I try to get ahead of myself. I buy a stash of stamps to keep ready for last-minute postings but the price goes up and I have to scramble for extra stamps to make up the difference.

Every time I try to plan meat-and-fish and vegetable-buying for the week ahead, something happens to put the kibosh on. One or several of us get sick. Or someone eats out during the day or has a big lunch or isn't hungry or there are lots of leftovers, or exhaustion and overwork means little desire to cook (where in these meal plans is there room for leftovers, which box do they go into?) and meat bought goes out of date and into the bin.

I go to the launch of *Miscellany 50*, the anthology I contributed to. It's lovely to listen to the readings, drink wine awkwardly with one hand, holding the doorstopper of a book under the oxter of the arm of the broken hand. I meet the New Island editorial director Aoife K. Walsh who asks about the novel I'm working on. Wow. This is the first time that I run into someone at a literary event who asks to see my writing. It makes me see how being at home because of pregnancies or kids or working early mornings is not helping this side of a writing career, the chancy side.

Things/people my children have mistaken for me:

> Mao Zedong.
> An orangutan.
> The bear from *We're Going on a Bear Hunt.*
> Theresa May.
> A conker.

I do an interview about my first novel for a podcast. It's been years since I've done any media stuff for this book and I'm a bit ragged. The interviewer observes that *Eggshells* is full of references to Celtic myths and legends and asks about my fascination with them. I'm not that interested in them, I say, confused by the question. I try to pad out my response but I can't invent an interest in fairytales that I just don't feel. A while after the interview, I'm getting a book from the bottom shelf in my sitting room when I come across many, many books on myths and fairytales, Celtic myths, world myths, tellings and retellings of fairytales. I had completely forgotten my previous obsession. *Eggshells* had been written eight years earlier, it's as if a different person in another lifetime had written it, a stranger.

During these years, the fallow years after events for the first novel have fallen away and before finishing my second, I'm quietly cleaning and having children. I do the occasional event, attend the odd book launch of a friend, but I'm not constantly out and about on the literary scene. A few people ask me, Where did you disappear to, where did you go? I'm baffled; I hadn't gone anywhere.

My family of origin has grown from six to seventeen, including partners and kids. There are eight children under seven so at family gatherings, conversations are frequently started only to be stopped when a child falls or cries or needs toileting. The unfinished anecdotes or stories part-told are like the half-eaten bowls of pasta scraped into the bin. Leaving each other's houses is like one big car boot swap event: I give my sister magazines I'm finished with, my mother doles out tubs of homegrown tomatoes and apples, months-late birthday presents are swapped, borrowed books are returned, snippets of interest cut from newspapers are given to the relevant person. My parents regularly find a reason, often obscure, to slip me a card with a few fifty-euro notes and the suggestion to buy myself a gúna. The dress is rarely bought but the sentiment is heartening: this money is used for treats and extras.

A letter arrives with a date for my daughter's hip operation. I try to feel grateful that her hips will be sorted before adulthood, that the issue was caught early, but really I feel deflated. Somehow I'd hoped the hips would magically right themselves, and after her ankle surgeries earlier this year, I'd hoped she was done with the knife.

That evening I check emails on my phone as I'm cooking dinner. Someone from the Lannan Foundation asks for my phone number; she says she has good news. I'm stirring a pot with one hand, trying to get butter and flour to mix with milk for macaroni cheese, and I google the Lannan Foundation with the slowly healing fingers of the other. At a quick skim I find something about residency programmes for writers in New Mexico. Ah, I think, with a toddler hospital stay coming up, this isn't doable. I resign myself to a, No, I'm sorry, not at this time conversation and send her my phone number. Later that night Martha calls. She asks if I'm sitting down, I say yes, why? She says she read my shocked response to winning €10,000 for the Rooney Prize and this is a whole lot more. Oh? She explains I've been awarded a Lannan Fellowship, worth $100,000. I am winded speechless. I can't take it in. A foundation I've never heard of with secret judges whose identities I'll never know is giving me a colossal, life-changing sum of money. Now all thoughts of my daughter's surgery leave my head: hips, schmips.

Martha asks if this will allow me to give up work. No, I say, I need to keep the job. She asks what I'll do with the money. I almost weep when I tell her, childcare. I had the baby on a waiting list to start crèche in two months' time. I had been mulling on it and almost decided it wasn't financially viable, me working as a cleaner, barely or not writing at all, and paying for two kids in crèche. It didn't add up. My partner had faith in my writing but I couldn't figure out how to justify the money. Suddenly the next few years opened up, a physical space spread wide open in my brain for writing time, slots of dedicated, scheduled writing time after work. I could keep my cleaning job and my hours of freedom to write. Sitting on the sofa after the call, I'm dazed with the news. I go upstairs to tell my partner; he's in bed with his back injury, and we cheer quietly, the baby asleep in the cot beside him. The house cannot contain me, it's too late to gather friends or get a babysitter and go out, so I go for a giddy walk that turns into a lep and a skip in the dark. In my family WhatsApp group, I announce that a woman from New Mexico has just given me a hundred thousand dollars. My siblings and parents warn me not to give my bank account details to strangers, to cop myself on (If it seems too good to be true, Caitríona, it *is* too good to be true). It takes a while to convince them this is legitimate.

I don't get round to buying anything with the money. I regard prize money as earnings that buy time to write. If I had a decent salary or lots of money from book sales, maybe this would feel like a windfall to fritter happily away on extras but it isn't, I need to save it. I do the maths of childcare for two children until school age and it more than covers it. A dream come true, if I'd known to dream it.

In my domestic arithmetic, I calculate childcare subtracted from my income, the income of the lower-earner in the relationship. My wage is the one that's discretionary, potentially give-up-able. If childcare fees are more than the lower-earner's wages, then it might be worth taking a hit for the expensive more-than-a-mortgage early years of childcare fees if you're aiming to progress in a career, but in my case, the home economics make no sense. There's no indication that my writing is improving with age or experience; in fact the opposite: my writing takes a hit with lack of time and sleep and consistent effort.

A few days later, I meet a friend for lunch. He usually insists on paying and I have to be sneaky to get there first, but this time he lets me pay after he hears my prize news. He's very happy for me, then, understandably, asks what I'll do with the money. I'll just write, I say. Write what, he asks. Try to finish my second novel, I say, but as I say it the words feel hollow. If I've struggled with the novel till now, how will I suddenly get better at it? It'll pay for childcare while I write, I say weakly, but I'm unnerved by the impossibility of explaining myself. Is this a nonsensical way to live, using a massive sum of money to pay for time to write something that may or may not be published, and which, if it is published, may or may not sell? Like ploughing money into a potentially non-viable business without first doing up a business plan. As an investment, it's a dud.

Minor nuisances with these feather-light sleepers become major. A blocked nose or a slight cough become reasons for staying awake for hours, either fraught and crying or giddy with Calpol relief. My daughter hates the sound of rain at night, my son hates wind. So a night with (rain + wind) x (sniffles + cough) = no sleep.

When I'm asked to provide something online, a blog post or interview or upcoming details of an event, the editor or event organiser usually asks for a photo. If I can't get to the laptop or it slips my mind, by the time I send on a current photo, the reply comes that they've already found one. And my heart sinks because I know the one they'll likely have picked: the black-and-white portrait done in 2014 when I realised I would need a headshot for this writing lark. It's posed and pouty and not the me I know, I wouldn't get those shots done today. Also, years have passed since those pictures were taken, with a significant amount of wear and tear in the meantime, and it feels disingenuous, like politicians who use decade-old posters at election time.

I'm asked to give a talk at a fancy lunch of a school parents' association to discuss my writing. I have burn-out, a confidence crisis, exhaustion trying to manage too many things. I turn down the offer. I get a brief urge to deliver a PowerPoint of Cif versus Domestos and tips on deep-cleaning mouldy grouting. I would like to have the courage of my ridiculous notions.

I get an email from the producers who bought the option to *Eggshells*. I'm given guidance on screenwriting and then told to get going and submit a first draft. This is so new it's overwhelming and thrilling at the same time. I download the cheapest version of screenwriting software I can find, which turns out to be incompatible with that of the producers and causes unwitting hassle. I buy several books on how to write screenplays and they make wonderful sense until I try to put the theories into practice.

I write a draft of the first act and submit it to the producers, it comes back with pages of corrections and I go back to it again. There's a Screen Ireland competition for funding and this is the goal, to get a decent first act in submittable shape. With each draft of a novel edit, there's an upward trajectory of improvement; progress can be seen. With each draft of the film script, it hasn't necessarily improved, just changed. It can sometimes feel like a cut-and-paste mash-up from different drafts, a clamour of different voices. I like the group chats, the camaraderie compared to the aloneness of novel-writing, but this style of writing comes much harder for me. My writing veers internal, and the struggle is to make it external, to make it all about saying not thinking. I write on Fridays, when my parents come to mind the baby, and I write in the evenings, when the children are asleep.

Although completely new to me, writing a screenplay seems less daunting than going back to my old *Wunderland*: starting afresh is the joy.

When she's two and a half, my daughter has hip surgery and is in a brace for three weeks. She's in terrible pain at night; it's vicious that after being sliced in two, all she can take is toddler paracetamol or ibuprofen. I stay beside her bed, the child on her back in a forced frog-leg pose. There is no sleep. She catnaps for an hour here, an hour there, the pain wakes her and after Calpol, she's giddy and ready for fun until the pain hits again. She can't burn off energy running around, so sleep hasn't a chance to take. We stay up, reading books, watching *Peppa Pig* on Netflix. For years, I associate Peppa with the child's recovery from her various surgeries and hate the theme tune irrationally. Somewhere in the middle of this recuperation, I go to a friend's book launch, my only foray into the adult world. I sit, sipping wine as if I've been released from some kind of cage, agog that this whole book world is going on outside of my Peppa + Calpol bubble. I feel a kind of sensory overload at all these people, all these words, as well as a simmering glee that the outside world still exists, and with poems.

I get my passport renewed. The photos from the booth show up a pair of black half-moons under my eyes like the under-eye patches American footballers wear on game day. I keep looking at the four replicated photos, foolishly hoping the next one will be different. The My Declaration section of the online form asks: The photo I have provided is my true image: Yes or No. It seems not so simple as all that.

For years, I've been talking up the plot of *Wunderland* to interviewers and to kind, curious family and friends who inquire, but I'm uneasy with all this talking and not enough doing. It can seem precious to say I don't want to talk about it. The poet Lavinia Greenlaw describes this: 'First I learned not to talk about it because others might be bored or alarmed, and then I discovered that I wanted, and needed, to keep my words to myself. If you share your words too quickly, they don't have a chance to gather their true meaning.'

I'm easily swayed by the asker's lack of enthusiasm or doubt, or conversely, if the response is enthusiastic, it feels like accepting praise for something that's not yet written. I can veer towards congratulating myself complacently for my words uttered instead of working at writing these words down.

I try tweaking the novel again when my broken hand is near-mended and I'm able to type gently. Five years is way too long to spend writing a novel, especially when the shift from child-free to childed has changed my brain so hugely. The parent part of my brain (distracted, reactive, watchy, practical, emotey) is at odds with the slower, deeper writing part. Also, starting a writing project is the fun part; I could start many books, stories, essays and power through on excitement and novelty for months. The hard part is sustaining it, and finishing takes gargantuan willpower, like trying to get builders to come back to finish the final touches of a job. (Finishing a book requires so much caffeine and sugary treats to keep me at the laptop that my weight surges towards the end of the writing project. I can probably connect various dental cavities to the end of book projects.)

There's a clandestine sweetness to writing a first novel, a newness and excitement. Furtively writing your first novel is like the early weeks of pregnancy, nursing your little secret. Parts of this second novel I know off by heart but I'm too close to see if it's good or bad. Eventually I hand it over to my agent who sends it out to a first tranche of publishers. It's not so much finished as gouged of all meaning, I can do no more with it.

The first couple of rejections for this too-long-in-the-writing novel are gut-punchers. I get an awful land when the publisher that had first option rejected it. I'd assumed acceptance was virtually a given and I was already thinking of using this deal as a bargaining tool if other publishers were interested. That's surely the definition of hubris, a lesson in cockiness.

The second rejection feels more personal, from an editor who expressed huge interest on first reading, gushing about exclusive world rights, but she couldn't sell it to the publicity, sales and marketing teams on account of my sales record, which is grim. I understand that and I'm annoyed at myself for believing the enthusiasm, for not keeping hold on my expectations. The rejections dribble in then and get easier with each one, I'm back into familiar territory. I compile the feedback into a file so I can learn from it, but all of the feedback about the actual writing is so subjective it's contradictory and hard to learn from. Some editors like the female character's narrated chapters and don't like the brother's, others feel the opposite. There are heartening words about my writing but the only consistent theme – as with my first book – there isn't enough plot, it's not commercial enough, how could they sell this, it's too quiet. My novel has no ta-da moments or zeitgeisty characters or commercial potential, but still, a book being called quiet feels odd. And quiet seems to be a negative thing in publishing; loud is what sells.

I have no reach, no social media following, no influence, no media connections. I naively thought that trying to get published a second time after proving my worth with some prizes would be easier, but it's harder. I'm not an exciting young debut, nor am I a seasoned consistent high-seller; I'm a middle-aged second-timer who has shifted few copies of a first book five years ago. I'm confident in the quality of my writing but am aware that the actual writing is only part of what is being sold. I am being sold and I'm not very sellable.

I try to keep in mind Lorrie Moore's words on rejection: 'So much about having a manuscript accepted is just out of your hands: the blood sugar level of a reader, the slant of light across a page, some personal event in an editor's life that connects them profoundly with something you've written on page three. Who knows? There's nothing you can do but write the best book you can.'

The randomness is both thrilling and terrifying, encouraging and discouraging. I think of my writing teacher's advice, just before I published my first novel: Never get too high or too low. If you're elated by a good review, then it follows that you'll be devastated by a bad one. In Eduardo Galeano's *Football in Sun and Shadow*, he writes of Albert Camus being a goalie for the University of Algiers soccer team: 'He learnt to win without feeling like God and to lose without feeling like rubbish.' Oh for such stoicism.

Things I find in my pockets or bag after being out with the kids:

Feathers.
Stones.
Sticks.
Leaves.
Shells.
Dead insects.
Peeled-off stickers.
Broken toy parts.
Coins.
Clumps of grass.
A dead bird's beak.
(Ingredients for a witch's brew).

Winning prizes gave me two good things (a boost in confidence and money) and one bad thing (a sense of dread). Both the Rooney and the Lannan were prizes for potential: rewarding what has come before, yes, but more so for showing promise. In a commercial sense, I have not gone on to do better things. In a review of Bette Howland's books, Elaine Blair considers the significance of Howland's prizes: 'And what bearing does it have, really, that Howland won the Guggenheim and MacArthur fellowships? These are merely bets placed on a writer's future. It's by the finished work that we judge a writer when her career has come to an end.' (That 'merely': ouch.)

Usually when something goes wrong in any part of my life, I let myself get in a heap about it, do a bit of wallowing, then clamber out and try to think what to do next. This time the clambering-out bit feels more difficult, but there's more distraction from rejection this time round because life is more chaotic. The children are very small, my partner's mother is gravely ill, I can't dwell too long on writing disappointments when there are so many pressing real-world needs.

THAT CHRISTMAS, MY DAUGHTER IS TWO AND the baby is eight months old, recently ensconced in crèche. Like his sister before him, he practically jumped out of my arms on his induction week and sobbed when I picked him up. These children thrive on new things, moving things (vigilance is required around running water and traffic, they move towards motion at speed) and I can only move so fast and be so new. Parents are invited to the toddlers' Christmas party in crèche one morning: I go, take her to Santy, eat treats with her. Then, when the party is over, I explain I'll be picking her up in two hours, Mammy has to work. She cries, clinging to my leg. Her favourite minder unclasps her and takes her off to the toddler room. I wait a couple of minutes, fighting back tears, then crawl along the floor to peer in the window. She's happily playing peekaboo around the minder's legs with another child. Even though I know she's content and entertained, I feel wretched.

I take my crumb-flecked knees to a nearby café to work on an essay, due that evening. I sit in front of the laptop trying hard to focus on the work but nothing will come, all I can think of is her crying face, her voice, *Mammy*. I wonder what it's all for. A physical wave of *What the hell are you doing* comes over me. Why pay for childcare so I can write, when the child is unhappy? No matter that I saw her content, that the crèche sent a photo of her playing happily to reassure me, I feel bad. If I'd vats of confidence in my writing, then this would make sense. I think of Annie Ernaux's words about leaving her mother in a nursing home in *I Remain in Darkness*: 'I am accumulating tonnes of guilt for the future.'

And yet ... when the first instalment of the Lannan prize money goes into my account, I look at my bank statement online. I blink at it but the numbers stay the same. I have never had so much money.

There are times when I catch myself absorbed in something ridiculously finnicky, I find myself thinking of my mother and grandmothers and generations of mothers on the tree rooted under me. The absolute extra-ness of what I'm doing, so far from need, the complicating of life for child-whims. Like trying to clean a plastic curly straw. No straw brush (I only recently discovered such things existed) can get into the curls and loops so after soaking the straws in a basin of sudsy water, I find myself sucking up the soapy water before blowing it forcefully back out many, many times until the remains of the chocolate milk have been forced through the loops.

The week before Christmas, an email arrives from Aoife at New Island about seeing my work. Oh the thrill! I try to mute my hopes and reply that I'll send it to her, admitting that I'm not convinced of it yet. In January, I email her again, sending on the manuscript and writing, 'I'm proud of the book, I think it's stronger than my first one, but I really don't know how to describe it (or market it, from your perspective!)' I end with, 'I'll stop talking now before I shoot myself in the foot.'

I read about the bittiness of Alice Munro's attempts to write while one of her children was in school and the younger one napped, her discomfort telling unannounced visitors she was trying to work. And then even when she rented an office, she was interrupted by a talky landlord. Like the use of a room in a gallery my brother once gifted me for Christmas. A man who also used the room was fond of telling stories, endless stories on repeat, while I was typing away trying desperately to write myself back into my novel. When I told him I only had a few hours to work before picking up my daughter, he would look aggrieved and say he was only trying to keep me company and he'd just tell me one more thing …

Going back to work after an extended maternity leave in January 2020, there's a noticeable increase in employment, the Luas is more crowded. The occasional morning, there's an incident on the 5.30 a.m. Luas involving people who've been drinking all night and are carrying it through the other end, or people waking up in dire need of various substances. I get talking to a carpenter from Roscommon about Connacht football, our kids. I get chatting to a few cleaners, a woman who works in a warehouse, a security guard. One woman asks what church I attend: to avoid being subjected to an attempted pre-dawn conversion, I name the church closest to my house and quickly change the subject before more details are required.

In early February, Aoife mails to say that New Island are interested and suggests meeting for a chat. We arrange a meeting in a hotel in mid-February 2020. Keep a hold of the hopes, I tell myself, it's just a chat. But I can't help feeling a tingle of possibility: this is the furthest I've gotten.

If somebody wants to complain about a worker, cleaners are an obvious target. We wear uniforms and move around in public spaces and are therefore highly visible when we stop to chat to co-workers. Desk-workers can tut about lazy cleaners hanging around yapping because their computer-based skiving is less obvious, their hours scrolling shopping sites or news or social media can go unnoticed. Also, when people complain about cleaners, they can be fundamentally complaining about a system that doesn't hire enough cleaners to do the amount of cleaning the complainers would like to see done.

Cleaners can be viewed as either superhuman or subhuman, even by the same person. We can be ignored and passed in corridors as if we don't exist, but left with heaving refuse sacks filled to the brim with papers and journals that no human could carry. I concoct angry signs in my head, signs that I never write, signs that I try to unsuccessfully shoehorn into my second novel, forcing my own progressively angrier thoughts into the voice of my character. 'We are cleaners not mules; please don't overfill the bins.' 'Please throw your rubbish *into* the bins not at the bins.' 'Have some basic respect, ASSHOLES.'

There's a sign in a lecture theatre in my building asking students not to eat or drink and to please dispose of any rubbish. Someone has written 'TLDR' on it. I explain to a less-online co-worker that it's an acronym for 'Too Long Didn't Read'; she asks how students can sit through a fifty-minute lecture but find a fourteen-word sign too long to read.

On TV shows, ads, films, there's a clichéd image of parents checking their kids at night and lovingly tucking a blanket around them; I can't do that. I can only tiptoe past their door and peek in. If I go in and smooth out their blanket or kiss them, the boy's head shoots up like a jack-in-the-box, he's standing in seconds, rattling the bars of his cot reaching for me with a *MAMAMAMAMAMA!* She's up and out shouting *Plaaaaayground NOW!*

A performance of my Starboard Home piece in the Pumphouse in Dublin Port is mooted. On a Zoom call with some documentary film people, one of them observes that my piece is only eleven minutes long; could I just perform something else as well? How do you mean something else? They are vague, it could be something I've already written or maybe I could just write something new about Dublin. Last-minute suggestions and casually conceived plans thrown out there with a 'just' break me out in hives, like when cleaners are asked to just ... I mutter something about having a look through my files, knowing well I've no bottom drawer full of Dublin-themed pieces. A meeting is arranged in Dublin Port to see the Pumphouse, currently a building site with heavy machinery. Hi-vis vests, hard hats and steel-capped boots must be worn, and a health and safety questionnaire must be filled out beforehand. I've been awake for twenty hours when I go online to answer questions I struggle to decipher: You are not allowed to stop a job if you feel it's unsafe: True or False.

I'll visit the venue for fifteen minutes, but I have to study statements like:

Only those trained in 'abrasive wheels' shall use any abrasive wheels such as con saws and angle grinders on-site. All excavations requiring access must be shored and battered. If you operate a fuel bowser, when not in use it must be parked on a flat, hardstanding area a safe distance from watercourses.

I can't drive a car never mind a digger or fuel bowser, but I commit to parking the fuel bowser on a flat area far away from water when I'm not using it. The event never comes about, but I've gained a knowledge of construction machinery so it's not been for nothing.

I love the language of construction, it all sounds so metaphorical and comforting: I'd like my house to be shored and battered. I've always been mildly curious about building sites, I have a sense as with a hospital or hotel or ship or port, of everyone doing completely different tasks that all fuse to form a smooth process. The logistics of these systems, the processes, fascinate me because I can't see bigger pictures, I clean my own patch of Trinity College and ferociously admire the people in charge of organising the cleaners and the caterers and the attendants and the lecturers and the admin staff and the gardeners into a massive institution that just works. I love reading my daughter's book about building sites with detailed diagrams of various machines and pull-out flaps to lengthen the cranes as the buildings grow. Near our house, I often stop the buggy at a block of apartments under construction to watch the builders at work. My daughter has so many questions about machines, questions I can't always answer, but the men working are kind and accommodating to these curious children and describe how rollers and pavers work. What fascinates the kids more than anything is the builders' portable cabins: the Portaloo, kitchen, and office, and if the Portaloo door is left open and they glimpse a toilet: day made.

Blackboards and chalk are used in the three lecture rooms I clean, long tin containers of hundreds of tiny chalk-stumps that I sort out at the end of term. The chalk sticks that are yellow on the outside and white on the inside remind me of Super Split ice pops, orange on the outside, vanilla ice cream on the inside. (I remember my college discovery that the same taste could be achieved by mixing spiced rum with fizzy orange.) It's satisfying work, deciding which stumps are too short to use, which are worth keeping, like sorting through my daughter's colouring boxes, sharpening pencils, dumping old crayon stumps, testing markers to see which work or can be used to make witches' potions.

One morning, just before cleaners finish and lectures start, I'm in the queue for the toilets. Two of the toilets are occupied by cleaners who are continuing their shouted conversation. Did that cream ever work? one of them shouts over the sound of pissing. It did a bit, the other one replies, it stopped the itching anyway but I still have the rash. I get the giggles but the students queuing are not amused. It reminds me of getting the flu vaccine in the health centre, cleaners and attendants mixed in with students. In the waiting room I met co-workers from the arts block I hadn't seen in ages. One had a conversation with me from the other side of the room about the birth of my first child; her daughter had just had an equally complicated birth. We were shouting across the room about episiotomies, haemorrhages, forceps, the students mouse-quiet among us. Twenty years ago, I would have been mortified about such things, I don't know if it's age or the openness of the women I work with or the let-it-all-hang-out-ness of having babies, but I've no self-consciousness about such chats. 'AND DID YOU TEAR OR DID THEY CUT YOU?' The female student beside me looks horrified but I can't stop, I'm locked into this compulsive birth-story-sharing. There were probably a lot of contraceptive requests that day.

A security guard in Trinity moonlights as an artist (or an artist moonlights as a security guard). He invites me to do a reading at an arts festival he helps to run in the midlands. I eat an enormous carvery roast beef meal in the hotel on Main Street before the event. It is heaven on a plate: three types of potatoes, almighty slabs of meat and a jug of extra gravy. The event goes well apart from a belly desperate to make itself heard, I talk louder to distract from my roiling digestion. The highlight, for me, is finding a large Dealz discount store near the venue and buying not just cheap sweets but also Christmas clothes for the kids. I almost miss the bus back to Dublin in my discount shopping frenzy.

Things I've found myself researching for books/stories:

The date of the abolishment of limbo for unbaptised Catholic babies.
The difference between a balustrade and a railing.
The name of the vehicle that carries a skip.
How quickly a fire starts and in what shape it spreads.
The shape of the map of Turkmenistan.
Where the concept of garden gnomes came from.
Discontinued brands of baked beans.

I regress hugely with the kids. I now say hostipal, I use singulars where there should be plurals, I say brang instead of brought, I were not I was. I go backwards while they go forwards. As my word-finding difficulties increase, their vocabularies increase. My memory is poor from sleeplessness, theirs are sharp. Their motor skills are better, their pincer grasps more dexterous than mine with its shoddily healed bones.

Rejections for *Wunderland* continue to dribble in sporadically. It's striking how much timing has to do with acceptance: if a certain editor is on maternity leave or about to change job or has already taken on a quirky novel too similar to mine (fulfilling the 'quiet' quota) then it's a no. I begin to see it as encouraging, what happens to the book is out of my hands. I have an image of my manuscript being flung around

Ireland and Britain before the pages gather up in an ordered sheaf and fall down the chimney of the right publisher.

There's a month that 2020 winter when the baby is ten months old, his sister is two and a half. For the next month both of them veer between vomiting and diarrhoea; diarrhoea and coughs; coughs and colds; colds plus or minus teething. I get the vomiting bug. Days are a conveyor belt of kids home from crèche sick, changing their clothes when they vomit, cleaning the carpet, sheets, duvets, pillows, only for it to happen again half an hour later. Nights I'm going between the two kids and the bathroom all night: I give up on bed and go to work. The world spins a bit differently when you're that tired. I'm clumsy with exhaustion and focus hard on not falling down stairs. The most arduous work is: mopping stairs and old wooden floors, hoovering lecture theatres with sparse electrical sockets. (So many pockets of time spent looking for sockets for the hoover plug as a cleaner is like the constant rummaging for soothers in a cot, I've spent years now scrabbling half-asleep around babies' cots for dummies.)

I go for easy wins when I'm tired: polishing brasses (satisfying shine, residual smell for proof of work done) and sweeping stairs. You can get away with dustier floors than dustier stairs: walking up a set of stairs, you see dirt at eye level. I'm so grateful for this job; I don't have to lead a class or perform surgery with a brain struggling to talk sense.

It's on the back of this month that I'm asked to participate in a panel discussion about the economics of being a writer, to be recorded for a BBC radio show. I thrust a crying baby at my partner when he comes home from work and I rush out the door. In the chaos of screaming children objecting to my departure, I forget to put on make-up. (This is the story of my early parenting years; tentative title for a memoir: *Forgetting Make-up*.) I tear into Boots to buy a mascara, rip up the stairs in Marks & Spencer to apply it in the toilets. My eyes hurt after being open for too long, the left eye twitches from too little sleep and too much caffeine.

I can see the irony of being incapable of debating the finer points of the economics of writing when I'm too tired and preoccupied with the practicalities of work and childcare, but I can't figure out a way to communicate this without sounding boring or bitter.

I sit as in a tutorial in college, eyes averted, hoping my name won't be called, feeling like a let-down for the audience who gave up an evening to come here, feeling like a fraud talking about writing when writing is the part of my life that is furthest from my mind at that point. I struggle to concentrate and miss cues, I answer the wrong question but I haven't the energy or speed to correct myself. At one point I fumble, saying I mean Leo Varadkar, but am incapable of elaborating or explaining my outrage at the country's leader who I believe prioritises high earners and disdains low earners. And … how to shift registers, how to go from Mammy to a group of adults to discuss real-world things; which world is more real?

My daughter pulls a copy of *Eggshells* off the shelf and says in an aggrieved tone, Mammy, no writing on books. Her father had shown her my book and told her that Mammy wrote it, she'd presumed I was writing *on* books as we keep telling her not to.

The TV show *In the Night Garden* has a character called Makka Pakka who carries a sponge and cleans all around him. I tell her Mammy is like Makka Pakka, I clean things in my job. She is most impressed by the physical jobs: truck driver, crane operator, builder, firefighter, bus driver; she doesn't know yet that cleaning is not respected. Will shame come, when she realises some of her friends' parents hire cleaners? I'll tell her my work is so difficult that some people can't do it, only people like Mammy can manage it: that might buy me a few years' respect.

Everything has been shifted to higher shelves because whatever is left on lower shelves or accidentally left on the table is grabbed and torn – bills, shopping lists are written over, keys and alarm clocks and jewellery are taken and hidden, some never found. The TV remote is taken and hidden so well we have no chance of watching TV that night after the kids are asleep. I sometimes wonder if they are trying to stop me having a brain-life outside of them. On a video call with my agent, I open my notebook to take notes of her feedback on an early draft of this book. There are scrawls on the page, I turn to a fresh page but that too has been written on, I keep turning and find the entire notebook has been scribbled on. I write my feedback notes in the spaces around the scrawls. My pens are taken, my sticky Post-it notes are taken and stuck to furniture, walls, my face while I sleep; bookmarks are shaken out of books.

I should mark the day I can leave a book on a table without it getting ripped to pieces, the day I can put the toilet roll in the holder without an Andrex puppy ad moment. The day I can leave my laptop down beside the sofa without it being mauled open, the screen locked from repeated crazed button-pressing.

In an office I clean there's a bust of Isambard Kingdom Brunel on a filing cabinet alongside a box of teabags and a bottle of hand sanitiser, which brings him down a bit. How do you get a Kingdom into your name? Could my kids get a County into theirs, even a Suburb?

One morning I'm cleaning the windowsills of a library under the eyes of distinguished-looking professors in gowns and robes in framed portraits. As I dust, I'm trying to figure out how many shopping bags I can carry from the Lidl on Aungier Street to the Stephen's Green Luas stop (four is the answer: one on my back, one in each hand, one on the left shoulder) and where can I get black-and-white polka-dot clothes for a *101 Dalmatians*-themed party for two kids by tomorrow. (Answer: nowhere. I buy white clothes and my partner paints black dots on them.)

I couldn't feel more different from the men in these portraits if they had fur and tails or scales. Imagine never having to think of housework or the admin of children (kid-min?), imagine working with no eye on the clock for picking up the kids, imagine how much you'd get done! But … I love getting to spend downtime with kids, I just want all of it. I want a few more hours to be squashed into my day, say four, a 28-hour-day seems reasonable (just for me obviously, if everyone got twenty-eight hours, more would be required of me). Or a new time zone just for my house; if every day could expand like those glorious extra hours on a plane crossing the Atlantic, the things that I could do!

I think of Philip Larkin's poem 'Afternoons', describing mothers in a playground: 'Something is pushing them/To the side of their own lives.' I enjoyed the middle life before I had children but now I love my side life following the kids around a park or playground; the side bit feels more middle these days.

Things rolling around in my head since having kids:

I keep meaning to …

I must get back to …

I have to charge ...
I must get batteries for ...
I must fix the ...
I need to find the ...
I'll have to look for ...
I must reply to ...
I must remember to pay ...
I need to book ...
I have to buy ...

Coming towards nine o'clock one morning in Trinity, just as we're finishing up our day's chores, large numbers of well-dressed women enter the building. A conference organiser bustles about, sniffing haughtily at the cleaners. I finish my last tasks and go to take my rubbish bags to the bin outside. They're gone. I look for them; another cleaner informs me that the conference organiser has stuffed them behind a door out of sight. I retrieve them and bring them downstairs (if I hadn't got them, I would be in trouble for hiding rubbish bags that would stink up the building). The groups of conference attendees coming up the stairs are unwilling to interrupt their three- and four-abreast conversations to allow me to pass. I give up saying, Excuse me! and just barrel downstairs with the bags in front of me like a smelly battering ram, which impels them to move.

The conference organiser is standing in the hall waiting to greet attendees. Her smile shrivels when she sees me going out the same door the women are coming in: maybe she had imagined invisible cleaners using a servants' entrance. I swing my bags into the large dumpsters outside the building, then go back in. Three more cleaners who work in the building converge in the hall. Have you ever seen a more ignorant group of people? one of them hisses. One woman asked me to carry handbag upstairs like I was her personal skivvy, she adds. I tell them about the organiser hiding my bin bags, another cleaner talks of being almost walked over as if she didn't exist. We agree we've never been treated with such disdain and outright rudeness. Who are they, we wonder. A poster on the wall announces a conference about the gender pay gap. We laugh at the good of it, the brand of white-collar feminism that doesn't recognise us as human never mind women. A mop-shaped blind spot in the gender conversation. It makes me think of Virginia Woolf's vocal support for middle-class women's right to vote in the early twentieth century, excluding the domestic servants as if they were subhuman. It didn't seem to cross Woolf's mind that working-class women deserved the same rights as their middle-class counterparts, the automatic obliviousness to the rights of those whose only function was to keep the middle-class women's houses clean and bodies fed while they campaigned for their own.

Bath-time in our house is not a relaxing wind-down part of the bedtime routine, but a manic activity in itself. I strip down to the minimals for this experience, which feels like high-energy aerobics in a steam room; maybe I could invent it as a new sport. For the bath-hour, I'm in a lather of sweat, running rags under my feet to stem the tidal waves rolling out of the tub to the soundtrack of wild shrieks and cackles, lunging for whichever child slips under the water after too ferocious a dive. Bath-time is tsunami-adjacent, a power of fun. Afterwards, I feel like I've lost pounds through sweat like a pre-race jockey.

I'm sitting opposite Marina Carr at a dinner after a writing event she read at; we're among the writers included in an anthology. I'm so awestruck I can't think of anything to say. I've just bought (another) collection of her plays to get signed but I'm so overwhelmed I can't find the words to ask her and don't want to gauchely produce the book. She assumes my partner is the writer and is surprised that it's me, I'm so quiet. I'm quite hard of hearing in noisy restaurants so nodding and smiling inanely is my usual demeanour. I tell her that her reading was nice. Such a feeble word, *nice*, like Kevin Costner backstage after Madonna's concert in her documentary *Truth or Dare* telling her the show was *neat*.

SOME DAYS LIFE FEELS LIKE A GUILT-RIDDEN BACKLOG of emails I haven't responded to. I work up the energy, drink coffee and reply to a glut of them, dust off my hands a job well done, then someone goes and replies immediately. Balls.

In the same way a shoemaker's child is poorly shod, a cleaner's house is not necessarily spotless. I run around my kitchen floor with bleach wipes to avoid taking out the mop and bucket. I use as few bowls as I can get away with, and brush crumbs off plates to reuse them rather than wash them. I read about a 2019 study that found that mothers spent on average two hours and twenty-one minutes a day cooking and cleaning and doing other domestic jobs. My figure is not even close. I prioritise the games and snuggles, the cleaning can wait. I maintain that I don't like to bring my work home with me.

My Trinity cleaning job is for large surfaces scrubbed clean without small hands yanking at the hoover wire or giddy feet skittering in piles of dirt. Sorting is my satisfaction at home: toy cars in one box, Lego in another. Containing things, at the end of the day, however briefly. Buying things to put other things into is a love of mine.

I love the paragraph about housework chores in Sebastian Barry's *Annie Dunne*, it's so satisfying to read about such arduous work, seventy years later in a kitchen fitted with every appliance necessary: 'I peeled the potatoes in the scullery, made the meals, scrubbed the tables, polished everything that could shine, brushed out everywhere, scoured, seared, ordered the larder under the stairs, killed the mice, banished the spiders, trapped the summer flies on fly paper, washed, dried, ironed, folded the clothes, the sheets and linens, went to my rest as tired as a wolf, as easy in my conscience as a lamb.'

One of the cleaners leaves a spare pair of knickers in a box in our tiny kitchen. Just in case, she says confidentially, you know the way after having a baby ... She trails off and we nod knowingly. I tell a friend about this glorious decency and forethought. Wouldn't it make more sense to leave a spare pair of trousers? she wonders.

I'm lucky to have co-workers and supervisors and a workplace so accepting. My pregnancy is welcomed, the baby celebrated, my pregnant or post-natal physical limitations tolerated, my new priorities accepted as natural. I don't have to hide my maternal feelings or pretend I have childcare sorted or act as if I don't have a child, like some mothers in the corporate world tell me. It's understood that I take holiday days last-minute if my child is sick, I'm told not to worry, mind myself and the child, it's only work. Novenas are said and candles are lit when the child is seriously unwell: the sheer decency of it.

I'm dithering uncertain about the novel I've just finished. I'm not even set on the title, 'Wunderland'; I can't decide if it's just a working title or if it's decent enough to keep. I feel a rattling unease about just how much editing is required to fix it. The rejections are an external disappointment, but more importantly, I'm not sure I believe in my book any more, and if I don't believe in it, how can I back it up?

The meeting with Aoife from New Island goes well. I trust her, she asks the right questions, sees the flaws but also the positives. The book requires substantial edits and major restructuring but there's hope. I come away from the meeting feeling optimistic with a backdrop of dread. The thought of going back to the novel, six years after I first thought it up, to put some shape on it, is daunting.

Ten days after the meeting, Aoife emails with an offer to publish. I feel an almighty surge of relief and joy. To feel that several people have responded to my characters, my invention, can never not be thrilling. But I'm also wary of the enormous amount of editing work required. I'm engaged in some frantic to-ing and fro-ing between accepting the deal or pressing the delete button on the novel file, when news of a new virus puts an end to my internal squabble.

When the country locks down, housekeeping staff in Trinity are put on a skeleton rota, working longer shifts on alternate days. In the empty college there's a sense of people having vacated the buildings hastily, like a post-apocalyptic, academic zombie movie. There are dirty plates and cups on desks with mouldy leavings in them, oozing and seeping fruit on counters, milk with weeks-previous use-by dates in fridges. A bad smell comes up from the sink-drains due to disuse: the water bulges and spurts when I turn on the taps, like in a house after coming back from holidays. Clocks in offices stay at winter-time after the change to summertime. (I like cleaning rooms not knowing which time is the right one, it goes with the general sense of discombobulation.) Diaries on desks remain open on March pages for months: I wonder if those tasks were completed, the phone calls and emails sent that needed to be sent, or seemed to be needed to be sent. There's a guide to film listings in the Irish Film Institute on someone's desk.

Carpet moths breed rampantly in unused areas, every footstep releases a puff of them. There's an unnatural stillness and stuffiness in the building: the stone stairs to the basement turn black with mould – not enough air is circulating to kill the damp. In an engineering lecture room, the desks are left in semi-circular formation, with chalked equations on the blackboard. Cleaners are not supposed to wipe blackboards but normal rules do not apply; I use the wooden duster to wipe away the engineering equations, feeling like a reverse *Good Will Hunting*.

One morning I'm one of only two passengers in the entire Luas, all the way to Trinity. At the stop I find myself repeating the strangely poetic rolling announcement: 'You may be asked to get off a tram or not to get on a tram if the tram is full.'

I go to the arts block on my break one morning to pick up a letter saying I'm an essential worker in case I'm stopped by guards. The arts block is spookily empty, only the attendant is in his cubicle the far end – we wave at each other like a greeting of fellow explorers across an Arctic wasteland. I get a bag of crisps from the vending machine for my break; if breakfast is at 5 a.m., 9.30 is lunchtime.

In the museum building, we work double shifts singly. Every time I unlock this beautiful building with its huge old iron key and use my phone-light to find the hidden light switches, I think how lucky I am to see an eerie place like this on my own, it's supposed to be haunted as any decent old building should be. Before the pandemic, a co-worker showed a photo of the white-robed ghost of the eighteenth-century murdered lecturer said to haunt this part of the college. It ruined some of the women for their solo Saturday shifts in the building; it added something for me. I hide a Toblerone and hand cream in a box under the kitchen counter for my friend working alternate shifts. She leaves sweets and bubbles for the kids, a cake and a magazine for me: what unexpected treasure, hard-got with most shops closed.

When the heat comes on at 7.40 a.m., thudding ticking trickling in clanky pipes, it's a marker of the day, the back of my work broken. Rooms are heated where nobody goes. I get to know the ways of the building, the cracks and creaks of old wood, the hiss and gurgle of pipes, the autoflush from the basement urinals at fifteen-minute intervals, the machines (photocopiers, computers, printers) that buzz into half-life when you dust them, the rhythmic thud of the huge pendulum in the hall clock, all watched over by the huge skeletons of the Irish elk.

One morning, the maintenance man comes in – the rarity of hearing another voice in the building! – and I tell him a bulb has gone in a kitchen, adding 'no rush to fix it', possibly the most superfluous thing I've ever said. After the spring cleaning is done, there's just dust to keep on top of. Staff members dribble back to collect items from offices when the first lockdown eases – it's almost a thrill to find rubbish in the bins. Now there's more spraying and disinfecting and preventative cleaning than any real work. At a certain point there's virtually no cleaning to be done and we're just cleaning over clean, as a co-worker puts it.

Crèche closes in the first lockdown. I go to work in Trinity, come home to mind the baby and two-year-old for the day, then when they're asleep at 8.30 or 9 p.m., I start work on my screenplay. The deadline for the Screen Ireland competition is weeks away and I need to get going on the first acts.

There are nights I sit at the desk trying not to sob with exhaustion. It's too much: part-time cleaning job, full-time childcare, part-time writing. The kids are discombobulated being out of their routine and have decided sleeping really isn't for them. I write at the desk instead of my usual bed-perch because if I'm near a pillow I'll be asleep. I scour the fine print of the film contract for act-of-God exit excuses but there's no mention of pandemics and crèche closures, I'm as locked in as I'm locked down.

Reading books and writing notes on how to write a screenplay while writing it feels the wrong way to do things, like reading a recipe as a half-arsed cake goes in the oven. I type fast to trick my brain into working fast, to outrace the sludge. Trying to dredge up new scenes, come up with writing that's fresh and funny or solutions to plot-holes when not only is my brain dulled with exhaustion, it's utterly devoid of imagination from a day of mediating battles with the kids, acting as a human shield between small fists and an even smaller target-head. Playgrounds are shut, my pair are too small to kick around a football or ride a bike or play a game together so the main amusement is me throwing the kids up in the air in turn. By the end of the day, my back is in ribbons. I bring toy diggers and tractors to the grounds of Grangegorman and try to pass off ruts and dents of gravel and sand as a beach; my daughter digs while the baby crawls quickly for a steep flight of concrete steps, trying to fling himself down. I lower the parenting bar from entertaining the kids to keeping them alive.

Grangegorman Psychiatric Hospital is now a technological university and an occasional Covid testing centre, a kind of health full circle with a pit-stop at education. I like places that dramatically change function: Jervis Street Shopping Centre used to be a hospital, Des Kelly Carpets in Phibsboro used to be a cinema, and a nearby red-bricked solicitor's office used to be a church. I like the notion of ghosts in ill-suited clothes awkwardly haunting these places. Daffodils appear in Grangegorman in December, which I attribute to disgruntled ghosts. It messes with time, thinking of Christmas while spring juts out of the soil.

The two-year-old is in a constructive phase, building fairy-houses and towers from blocks. The baby is in a destructive phase, knocking everything with manic glee, thrilled at these constantly appearing buildings just for his amusement. The toddler beats the baby, the baby cries, the mother shouts then feels terrible for raising her voice.

My daughter has an imaginary friend called Doom from mishearing talk of Zoom calls – seems apt if slightly ominous.

If one more person says of lockdown, *We all have so much time to think*, I'll lend them my kids for an hour or two. I share a manic cackle in a park with another mother as we set our toddlers running up and down a hill shouting, 'Two metres, two metres apart!' I'm wrangling the baby away from lunging off a high ledge, kamikaze-style. 'Bored!' the mother shrieks in near-hysteria, 'I'd give my eye-teeth for bored!'

Words I'd never heard used before: furlough, sourdough starter, Zoom, Joe Wicks.

An Irish magazine runs a feature about surviving lockdown, which includes the tip: 'Keep the cleaner. You still have a full-time job!' It reads as if the cleaner is a vaguely useful possession. There's no explicit snobbery in the article, just the assumption that the person reading is a woman in a job that pays well enough to hire a cleaner, and that her leisure time is of the greatest importance. There's a prolonged social media spat in the UK over whether people should be allowed to bring their cleaners back to clean their homes during lockdown. More thought seems to be put into whether their dog catches Covid than their cleaner.

When playgrounds reopen, I do a little victory dance with another mother in a local playground, our children ecstatic at the unlocked swings and slides. I go early in the morning, pushing both kids on the toddler cage-swings, my arms pumping alternately, my son shrieking delightedly, my daughter roaring *Higher, Mammy!* I push them for an hour, longer sometimes, the children contained and entertained, the holy grail. And I can stand still, make like a donkey and semi-sleep standing up.

Sometime in the middle of lockdown, both children get headlice. There's also a greenfly infestation in the garden, swarming all over windows, on the clothes drying on the line, our faces. Then a large cockroach somehow lands in our bathroom. I google 'Getting rid of cockroaches / head-lice / greenfly,' thinking of Annie Dillard's word 'teemingness'. To prevent cockroaches every drop of water must be mopped up in a bathroom. To get rid of headlice, clothes, bedding, soft toys all need to be washed. We delouse the kids, scour every bit of lint, grain of rice, breadcrumb for movement; I'm never without my magnifying glass looking for tiny legs. There's potty-training at the same time; I'm never not cleaning, never not itching. The lice are resistant little fuckers, defying multiple delousing treatments. I research and discover they play dead when hair is washed but they're in a state of suspended animation, biding for time until they can get going again, like so many dormant volcanoes. How *sinister*. A vet of my acquaintance gives me a bottle of flea ointment: problem solved.

Close on the heels of the greenfly and headlice infestation, a mouse – or what I casually think of as 'a' mouse – appears, crunching on raw pasta behind the wall – it seems almost like company. It becomes an infestation very quickly. Humane mouse-traps don't work, traditional mouse-traps work sporadically. We box up all food, wipe every crumb from every surface, sweep up every bit of food as soon as dinner is eaten, starving them out. I leave the kitchen sweepings one evening to answer the call of a child and when I come back a minute later, there are several mice devouring the crumbs, scurrying back under the dishwasher when I run at them with the brush, feeling like the farmer's wife in the nursery rhyme.

That night, I'm sitting on the sofa when a mouse darts out between my feet. (I hate the suddenness of them; if they moved slowly I wouldn't feel quite the same revulsion.) I sit on another chair. Another mouse shoots out from that chair. I stand in the middle of the room holding my laptop with one hand, typing with the other, on a tight screenplay deadline for lunchtime the next day while mice emerge from behind the bookshelves, under the TV, from tiny gaps between the speakers. Starvation emboldens them, they stop hugging the edges and dart around the middle of the floor, desperate for food, I am standing lifting my feet in turn, trying to focus on typing one-handed in the midst of this plague. It's revolting but I have a deadline. This is one of those moments I look at myself and wonder how it has come to this, my younger self who might have imagined a writing life as more elegant, more sorted.

Foods Cabra mice like:

- Chocolate.
- Peanut butter.
- Cooked rashers.
- Tayto Cheese & Onion crisps: they hold no truck with generic supermarket brands. I imagine a promotional tie-in with Tayto, an ad jingle, eight out of ten mice agree.

I make the screenplay deadline with an hour to spare. The mice get caught, all eighteen of them, my partner doing the dirty work of trapping and disposal, careful not to show the kids who would want to keep the corpses as very still pets. I sign the contract with New Island, and feel a wave of relief followed by cautious pride. The book will be published. It's someone else's problem, off my screen and onto the editor's. I begin to feel curious about what a pair of fresh eyes will make of the manuscript, excited about the potential fixings. The process from early tentative discussions to signing the contract has taken four months, due to Covid and lockdown confusion as well as my own hesitancy. It feels good to have made a decision to push through and own the book. Despite my misgivings I want my writing to reach readers, otherwise what's the point? I buy an orange Le Creuset coffee plunger with some of my advance. It's a ludicrous luxury when I have a coffee pot already, but I feel like something ludicrously luxurious, and I want a congratulatory burst of orange when I drink coffee.

The editor assigned to work on my novel is busy with other projects so editing will start in autumn. I'm enormously relieved: autumn will hopefully bring crèche reopening and the chance of some functioning brain-power. I can now focus on cleaning + childcare and not force my brain into shapes it can't make. But I'm behind on a short-story deadline for a Dublin-themed anthology and force myself back to it. One night when the kids are asleep, I'm writing in the front bedroom when sirens start up. I look out to see huge gangs of drunk/coked-up teenagers spilling out of the park across the road in the throes of a large-scale fight, guards chasing them out. Lockdown has brought enormous teen raves to the park which can get messy. There are garda cars and vans, the garda helicopter hovers, teenagers running or hiding behind parked cars, so many guards but not near enough to manage the number of kids in various stages of punching the heads off each other. I'm too nosey and distractable to concentrate on writing, so along with our other neighbours I watch this live soap opera from the window.

I've always been swotty about deadlines, have never asked for an extension before and then delayed the extension. The editor of the anthology says to take as long as I like, that everything is suspended. I've been lucky with lockdown-timing, I haven't missed out on any book-related event or launch; my literary horizon was mostly blank to start with. Other writers, especially new writers, have had plans derailed, necessary public appearances stopped. With small kids and a stalled writing career, I was living my own private semi-lockdown anyway.

When I have no deadlines I love succumbing to the here-and-now-ness of small children. I love the hours-long dithering walks with short legs, stopping frequently to examine a gutter, hunting for Incy Wincy Spider coming down the waterspout. We inspect ladybirds on blades of grass, blow fluffy parachutes from dandelion clocks, dig houses for worms, but the only problem with observing nature in its minuscule perfection is it requires having children who can stay still. There seems to be some centrifugal force which propels my kids in opposite directions, giving me a split second to decide who's in the most imminent danger before they spread exponentially further apart. Excuses I'd give later go through my mind: yes I know I let the baby crawl into the canal, Guard, but I was trying to grab his sister who was running at cars and more certain death.

When I try to write, I'm listless and unfocused. I just want to clean and sort and tidy and get the house in order. Cleaning can help you feel like you have control over something uncontrollable, like a coronavirus. A year ago, when my daughter came home from hospital after her infection, a nurse called to supervise me giving the first IV dose of antibiotics so before she was discharged, my partner and I took turns on our trips home from hospital to scrub and disinfect the house thoroughly, ostensibly for the nurse's visit, but maybe for ourselves. Maybe, I thought, if I'd done this when the child got chickenpox, it might not have turned into sepsis.

I feel disconnected from the writers interviewed about their lockdown experiences who are gazing out on lush mountain streams and thinking deep thoughts: where are the writers living in small houses with pocket-sized gardens and a non-desk day job and small children, desperately trying to come up with two separate activities that a baby and toddler can do and not kill each other? The notion that this is a nice time to take up online yoga and learn an instrument and mindfully drink tea (made in a teapot with real tea-leaves, of course, because self-care!) and stare out windows and compose the pandemic novel – this doesn't work when endless logistical and practical concerns take over.

One morning, I go into Trinity for a double cleaning shift. I'm overjoyed: I can escape my 2km limit, and it feels like cleaning is a rest compared to home life. I have set breaks and can drink an entire cup of coffee in one sitting. I get my keys from a security guard, whose kids overlap mine. He tells me I look very chipper, I say yes, I got four hours of uninterrupted sleep last night, I feel so good I woke up before the alarm. We whoop in joy, he has shoddy sleepers, he gets it.

Today's task is deep-cleaning the toilets. I do the men's first, the tougher job: this goes against my training but I need to reward myself with the easiest last. The urinals flush automatically every fifteen minutes so I time my work-day around that. There are four toilets and three urinals in the men's, and only three toilets in the women's, probably because women were let into the college as an afterthought. The men's toilets invariably stink. Decades of shoddy aim at the urinals means a stench that no amount of bleach can overcome. Urinal drains are often clogged with chewing gum, despite an open bin two feet away. I rush the men's, it's unsatisfying not being able to get near the bottom of the bang of piss, and the eye-burn of stale urine is unpleasant. The section in my cleaning manual on how to clean toilets includes, under the heading URINALS, 'Check the drain for obstructions and remove, using a tweezers.' I don't have a tweezers so I pick out the gum with gloved hands before binning the gloves. The Sanitary Fittings section for toilet areas of my cleaning manual states that the surfaces must be 'Free from debris/dust/stains/body fats/fluids and hairs.' Body fluids contains an unfortunate multitude.

After the deep cleaning, it's maintenance. Never have light switches and doorknobs been cleaner. Door panels that have been Brasso-ed are now cloudy with beaded dried drops from disinfectant spray. It's an unsatisfactory cleaning, it's all invisible, unprovable.

The National Library reopens after the first lockdown for those carrying out research so I head into the online catalogue. In my years of writing in the library, I've never ordered a book but I decide on Eavan Boland and Medbh McGuckian. These poets are my entry code to a desk in the library, but then reading interviews with them turns into procrastination, a way to avoid writing, even if it feels like a very real form of necessary research. I compulsively search for the how of juggling, the how of earning money and making books while spending time with your children. The constant struggle interests me more than the successful juggling, like McGuckian's answer to a question on whether being a wife and mother helped or hindered her poetry: 'When I'm balanced, the roles can be juggled evenly. I switch smoothly enough from the backseat of domestic responsibilities to the exciting driver's wheel of poetry. But I can't carry both things at once. The children have to be unconscious, asleep, before I can write . . . I fall off the wire about twice a week.'

I like the word unconscious, I need my children to be unconscious or elsewhere. How reassuring these poets are.

There is Covid in my daughter's crèche room so toddlers are sent home for a week. I abandon the laptop, relishing the opportunity to spend one-on-one time with her, so rare since her brother was born. One morning, we spend four hours in a near corner of the Phoenix Park, at the rockery near the pond. A park lodge that looks like a fairy-tale witch's cottage stands on top of a small hill with four sets of stone steps leading up to it. We spend hours climbing up and down those steps, stopping to examine worms (Do worms have eyes

Mammy, where is their bum? – more googling) and running from the witch's house whenever we see movement or smoke from the chimney. We're just inside the gates of this huge park, but our area feels like a pocket universe with endless puddle-potential. When we find acorns, I tell the child about squirrels hoarding acorns before sleeping for winter, then I doubt myself – is that a thing? Do some animals really sleep for an entire season? Lucky *bastards*.

Six months after the college locked down, students are back. Cleaners good-naturedly complain about them even though we're grudgingly happy to have a bit of normality again. Rolls of heavy-duty blue toilet paper and chemical spray are left out for students and lecturers to sanitise their own desks, and wads of paper are clumped around the bins, lobbed cack-handedly.

I FINALLY GET UP THE COURAGE TO WRITE ABOUT my daughter's illness eighteen months ago. I write about how chickenpox morphed into invasive Group A Strep infection, which randomly attacked her ankle joint and bone. I write about not knowing how ill she was getting at home because she was too small to tell us. I describe attempting to hand her over to a nurse in the rush to emergency surgery, the child pulling out my hair in her desperation to cling to me. I write about the many nights spent sleeping in a hospital chair by her bed, the second surgery, pregnantly rushing the length of the ward to vomit. I write about my bewilderment on hearing the word arthritis used, and the parallel world in which the words, 'It's only septic arthritis' were used to reassure. I describe administering IV antibiotics through her PICC line for another month at home. I write about the sign in the X-ray department saying a chest X-ray for a child emits the same radiation as a return air trip between

Rome and Dublin; I ask what about four ankle X-rays, an MRI and seven hip X-rays, has she circumnavigated the globe twice over in radiation terms? I write about the consultant saying if we'd waited another twenty-four hours to bring her in that we wouldn't be looking at this (when he watched her attempt a hop-along listy run on a subsequent check-up). I couldn't, and can't, bring myself to ask, What would we be looking at?

I'm given a full-page spread in a Sunday supplement. The piece is the rawest, realest thing I've ever written and it feels exposing. The aim is to draw attention to how preventable this particular infection is with the chickenpox vaccine (I hadn't known one existed until she got sick). It's the first time I've written something with an agenda, and after it's published I get nice feedback, some from parents whose children endured something similar, but I feel an emptiness. It can't be measured if a reader pays heed and vaccinates their child, it can't be noted if a child doesn't get very ill because they've been jabbed. It's a strange, waity sort of feeling, writing something with a purpose and never knowing the outcome.

I START WORKING ON EDITING *WUNDERLAND*. The editor is the perfect fit. We work by phone and email, I don't meet her because people are still clumping in family and friend groups away from virus droplets. She shows me the flaws, the chronological inconsistencies, the incongruities. She shows me the need to develop more structure and actual incident, to thwart my tendencies towards meandering plotlessness.

The edit takes ten months, partly because of the pandemic. I see from the email chain that there are continual stallings; the crèche sends my kids home because of case numbers rising or a close contact in their classes or a minder getting Covid. It's all so haphazard; my kids are so small that if they're awake I'm unable to work, and at least one is always awake. The editor is homeschooling her kids, and is hugely understanding.

It feels strange, trying to get my head back into a character I'd first imagined six years ago and figure out his motivations.

Sometimes I wonder what I was thinking when I came up with him, it's so difficult to burrow back into his brain. Naming him hasn't brought him any closer to me. I find myself watching videos on YouTube of flames spreading to research a fire scene in the book, and getting carried away with a new form of distraction: the speed of the flame-spread! Some of the videos have hundreds of thousands of views, must be some fetish I'm unaware of.

The first edit (or first pass) coincides with six weeks of a teething and/or sick one-year-old, pacing a box-room floor with an increasingly heavy child in my arms multiple times a night. The three-year-old is up every night at 1 or 2 a.m., trying to convince her that now is not the time to be going to playgrounds takes up to three hours. She won't be fobbed off with her books (I can't read, Mammy). I try so hard to focus on editing but I find myself emailing the editor with apologies and the teething-baby excuse. I get two hours' sleep too many nights and I don't know who I am.

Exhaustion compounds the enormity of the task and I procrastinate editing, I'll do anything but that. Here's what I will do:

Clean the toilet.

Clear out the food cupboard, rearranging tins of tomatoes alphabetically by supermarket brand and by consistency, chopped vs. whole.

Pull out the sofa to hoover behind it.
Upend the sofa to shake out the trapped pens/coins/food detritus.
Dust the top bookshelves perched on a stepladder.
Clean the stepladder.

I fantasise about laying my pages out on the floor of a huge empty warehouse and having the time and the physical space and the brain-space and the sleep to get a run at this, to really see the bigger picture and what needs to be done. Editing does not work by dipping in and out like this. At a certain flowy stage of the process, writing can be inched along by doing a bit every day, but a major restructuring requires big-picture thinking and more time and brain-space than I have. The editing requires an immersion I can't give it.

Years ago, I stayed in a small cottage by the sea for five days to work in solitude on my first novel. I had enough ready meals and bread and coffee to not have to shop for food or do any housework apart from washing my plate and cup and bowl. It wasn't just the mounting word-count but the total blissful immersion in my characters' world that made the writing fall into place after that.

A draft being emailed to your editor: the deliciousness of the enforced break while waiting for feedback.

My sister comes over to bake with the children while I try to constrain grabby hands determined to fist ingredients into mouths or mix together any old how. The whisk is used as a whacker, the rolling pin as a hammer, the sieve as a hat. The mess is joyous, the kids on the floor licking bowls and wearing the melted chocolate while my sister leans, dazed, against the counter: this wasn't how it was supposed to go.

When I clock into work after the October wintertime change, a security guard tells me that night-shift workers work an extra hour unpaid in October, while night-shift workers work one less hour on the night of the March summertime change. The clocks in the offices I clean have come the whole way around the summer and righted themselves; in the same way that a stopped clock is right twice a day, an unchanged clock is right half the year. Years ago I tried to explain the concept of daylight savings time to students in Japan even though it's only vaguely clear in my own mind; I muttered something about Scottish children coming home from school on winter evenings. My partner found himself trying to explain proportional representation in voting to Japanese students with very limited English.

Office staff are mostly still at home. Winter clothes hanging on the backs of chairs since March are seasonal once again. The heating is turned on in October; the carpet moths flare up again, tiny fluttering co-workers in the absence of humans.

The pandemic shows up the disconnect between my Trinity housekeeping role and former student role. An e-newsletter tells alumni that Trinity researchers are at work on the vaccine, reassuring 'us' that essential services like cleaning and maintenance are still happening, encouraging 'us' to stay safe. So the alumni part of me should stay safe at home while the cleaner part of me should keep coming into my job to reassure alumni that all is well. During a storm the following year, an email tells us the college will be closed the next day because 'your safety is the priority'. The same email tells essential Estates & Facilities Staff to make every effort to come to work.

Cleaners who worked the pandemic are given a €100 gift card. Such small money from such a large institution brings such happiness: we've been seen. We talk up ways to spend it, usually on something for the home or for somebody else in the family.

When it's said of someone in the college (a lecturer, the new provost, office staff): she wouldn't pass you, it's the highest compliment. They stop to acknowledge you as a fellow human being. Shouldn't be, that it needs remarking.

With cleaners back on the same shifts, I occasionally find myself in conversations that veer unpleasant. The anti-vax movement has swooped up various family members of my co-workers, who report back theories gleaned from Facebook. This gradually morphs into distrust of government who are believed to be prioritising immigrants and not looking after 'our own'. I try arguing that the anger should be directed at the government, which has failed its people on housing and not at immigrants but the government is too vague an enemy, and I'm outbursted at when it's (understandably) felt that I haven't a clue as I don't have a son or daughter on a housing list for years. If more compassion and general cop-on had gone into solving the housing crisis, then maybe the very real shortage wouldn't have sent decent people up against immigrants. Rumours spread about 'a wave of foreigners coming up from the back' of the college, mirroring the fear-stoking of the right-wing red-tops, but these fears have a legitimate starting point. Contract workers are being hired to do security guard work in the college for lower pay and fewer benefits than permanent staff members, replacing public-sector job security with private-sector precarity. If the lower-waged weren't so thoroughly and repeatedly screwed over by successive governments, if wages weren't so laughably insufficient to outweigh increased living costs, if renting a home was within the bounds of possibility for everyone, the far-right movement wouldn't have had such opportunity to take hold. I argue the worst of the racism then walk away when I can't make someone else see my side, and my side is so privileged I can see why it inspires resentment.

And yet ... through all this rhetoric there is a thorough and innate decency towards cleaners and workers from other countries, a practical inclusiveness at odds with the words.

Notions of racism don't meet the actions: when a cleaner from another country joins the crew, there is automatic acceptance. I've also found tolerance towards me, a more reserved person who can sink into herself in a crowd and offer little to group banter but laughter.

A lived, practical generosity in common. Easter eggs and Christmas and birthday gifts are left in my cubby for my children. Supervisors set up Christmas clubs to help the women put by money each week; some sell Mass cards at cost price. Anyone with experience helps to write letters or fill out forms for insurance companies and banks and council and government departments. Vouchers are snipped out of newspapers and passed on, newspapers and magazines and clothes are swapped around. A grand mucking in together.

I'm asked to give an online talk one evening on the theme of work for Trinity Long Room Hub. I write some thoughts on my attempts to balance my writing work with paid cleaning work and the parenting that seeps through the entire space. The children are downstairs with their father, aware their mother is in a meeting upstairs in the bedroom. They're used to their father being in online meetings; they object to their mother being so engaged. I give my talk and after the other speakers are finished, there are questions.

As one of the other speakers is answering a question, my son bursts into the room and clambers onto the bed beside me. His head appears on-screen so I raise the laptop.

He raises his head and I raise the laptop again. I'm now holding the laptop in the air with one hand and stretching up so my face is on-screen, looking like I'm trying to find the perfect angle to erase the double chins from lockdown overeating. I try to push the toddler's head a bit lower, but like a whack-a-mole, it keeps bobbing back up, two little eyes peering delightedly at himself on the screen. I give up and accept that the top of his head will be on-screen beside me, intermittently popping up to lean closer to the screen and smile at his own face like a meme of a monkey in the wild who discovers a camera. I'm asked a question and I answer it, the toddler is amazed to see me talking on-screen and pokes me in the side, shrieking and giggling.

There are sudden fast-moving footsteps and my daughter bounds in. She scurries onto the bed and starts jumping wildly, I try to steady the laptop. She dives onto the pillow, climbs up beside me, and puts her face right into the camera. I mute myself, try to pull her down with one hand and hiss like an irate ventriloquist, Stop, Mammy's working. But she just wants to see herself again, as does her brother and they surround me, jostling to get their faces on-screen and block me out. Meanwhile my son starts grabbing my stomach and squeezing it painfully, I try not to wince on-screen and hiss instead, Stop pinching Mammy. I raise the laptop to above neck level so I'm only visible from the chin up.

Now my partner appears at the door in shock, he'd been in the kitchen and hadn't noticed them escaping. He's hissing, Get out of here, Mammy's working! and crawling around the floor trying to stay off-camera, attempting to drag the boy off the bed by the ankles, but these kids have a taste for stardom now and will not be corralled. I give up all attempts at professionalism and giggle, grateful that the theme of my talk was the muddling and juggling, surrounded by two living embodiments of the not quite managing it all.

I do a brief interview for a Sunday supplement about my cultural preferences. I talk about my favourite song, 'Joyce Country Céilí Band' by The Saw Doctors. I mention my favourite line: 'Boomshakalakalaka buns and cakes.' I may never be taken seriously.

I bump into a neighbour who greets me enthusiastically and says what an exciting time it is. I agree, flattered that she's so supportive of my writing. She asks when it's all happening and I say it won't be until next year sometime, probably autumn. She looks astonished and says she thought they'd be more exact by now. I say Covid has delayed everything. She looks confused and asks, but what's that got to do with the baby? What baby, I ask. That baby, she says, pointing to my belly. Oh, I say, I'm not pregnant. Ah go on, she says with an exaggerated wink and a poke in the ribs, you're pregnant. I'm not, I say. She tells me one of her sons saw me walking down the street and he said I was definitely pregnant. I say

I'm still not. She says her other son saw me coming into the house and he said I was pregnant. I say there's no baby, it's just cake. She tells me another neighbour saw me coming down the steps and said I had to be pregnant. I almost agree that I'm pregnant just to stop the conversation.

I spend a long time, much longer than is wise, on a commission for a well-regarded journal. It's such an honour to be asked, I'm elated and put my all into it: this feels like entry into the literary establishment. But it's a struggle: I can't see the essay, I can't hold its entirety in my head like I used to. There are disjointed anecdotes that work fine on their own but don't fit together, there's no cohesive thread to make it whole. I don't know what's missing or how to figure it out.

The deadline approaches and I ask for an extension, then submit something that's not even close to my glorious intentions. An email comes, rejecting it. I'm absolutely flattened, I didn't think rejection was possible for commissioned pieces. It's a very decent email offering praise, but explaining that structurally it's not working and there's not enough time to fix it. I reread the email feeling gut-wrenching disappointment followed by shame: I thought publication was a foregone conclusion and I'd proudly told several people about it. The editor offers a kill fee, which I'd never heard of before, sounds so bloody and cruel but is actually a generous booby prize. My initial instinct is to salvage any pride and say a haughty no, but I spent so long on this thing that I accept the money, shamelessly.

I allow myself a day to wallow. I email my agent about the rejection to get it off my mind and see if she has any solutions. I rant to my partner, stop any writing work, and give myself a day of dossing and treats. I think it's important to acknowledge and go with disappointment and not push through sitting in dejected distraction in front of a screen.

My agent comes back with some suggested cuts. I'd written a 5,000-word piece, but cut 1,000 words off it and she submits elsewhere. It's published in a UK daily newspaper, the pay is decent and punctual. Then from the 1,000 words cut from the original piece, I spin a new essay and my agent manages to place that in a US literary journal. I would rather be published at home among my peers, but when that fails, I'll gratefully accept elsewhere.

Questions to ask myself:

Why do I write (what else is there)?
Why not give up (what else can I do)?
You shouldn't answer a question with a question but I don't have the answers. And like gambling, there's always a chance the next one will pay out.

AFTER THE EDITS OF *WUNDERLAND* I GATHER UP the folders of notes, the printed-out drafts with scribbled side-notes, the notebook of German compound nouns, the books of European train timetables, the refill pad of snag lists of things to fix, the random Post-its and scraps of paper panic-scrawled in the middle of the night (**FIX -**, **SORT - **) and the German–English dictionaries. It's a pleasant form of procrastination, to take a side-task and make it a main one. I put two of the dictionaries into a charity shop donations bag, and put the kept one along with my notes in a box and take them up to the attic. I dump all the notes into a huge plastic tub containing phrase-books for languages I never got round to learning (*Everyday Sesotho*, *Arabic for Beginners*). How did I ever think I would have the time?

Most of the notes I made for what turns out to be this book are in a tiny notebook I keep in my cleaning smock, or on paper I find in recycle bins. On these scraps of paper are also lists of things I have to do or buy. These age with the kids: nappies falls off the list after a few years. Jobs done and pencilled through are on the scraps: Sort hot press/sort kids' clothes for charity shop. Like looking at photos taken a year ago, how quickly children change, essential items become obsolete.

In a tiny patch of soil beside some flats near our house, someone has planted crocuses and primroses: a punch of colour among a mass of concrete can feel like a Versailles worth of flowers. In the park across the road, drug paraphernalia of syringes and burnt teaspoons has given way to silver bullets and balloons, very appealing to a curious crawler who tries to eat them, and to his sister for use as engines for her miniature spaceship. She orders us into our tree-branch seats, we clamber dutifully in and she flies us to the moon with impressive sound effects. Once we've arrived on the moon, we float around the grass until I'm scolded for my excess gravity, FLY MAMMY, FLY.

Wunderland is published in September 2021. It's an in-between time, a phase of Covid lockdown in which venues are permitted to host events of up to twenty-five people (including publishing and bookshop staff), socially distanced, no wine. My parents are not attending indoor events for health reasons, and inviting a handful of friends and family to watch me witter on behind a mask didn't appeal; offending people I couldn't invite seems like the worst part of organising a wedding. Instead, I do an interview in a bookshop that will go online at 6 p.m. on publication day. I can't bring myself to send round the link, to ask friends and family to finish their work weeks and go back to the screen to watch me pontificate on writing, without even a glass of wine thrown in. I send an email saying I'm not having a launch but to consider buying the book, not mentioning the YouTube interview, fully aware that my viewer numbers will be dismal. If you don't self-promote easily, it can be hard to raise figures or even care about raising figures. Instead of a launch, I have some lockdown-friendly treats.

My sister gives me a bunch of sunflowers, my favourite flower. I meet a friend for breakfast, a retired cleaner I worked with twenty years ago who took photos of me with my first novel in Hodges Figgis six years ago: less giddy glee now, more quiet pride. I meet another friend for lunch with a pint of cider thrown in: I stick to one pint because picking up toddlers from crèche drunk doesn't seem wise. When the kids are in bed I have a takeaway with my partner, feeling like the queen with multiple celebrations, my cup and belly full. Having such low-key celebrations befits a fairly dour book hard-got, and with small kids and a lowered tolerance for alcohol, I haven't got my party shoes fully back on yet anyway.

Epilogue

When I was writing it, I still believed that *Wunderland* could amount to something, that seven years of effort might pay off. To say it's a disappointment is an understatement: in commercial terms, the novel is a failure. Six months after it's published, *Wunderland* has sold 746 copies, a good many of them to my mother (who uses her maiden name when buying online in the belief she won't be recognised, never mind the 'Lally' on her credit card). The reviews are mostly good, the odd incorrect assumption or beef with my approach, but it's all part of the game, you need quotable review lines in order to apply for funding, get your next book published, etc. It doesn't feel connected to the actual writing.

Wunderland was nominated for no prizes, sold few copies, was translated into no other languages – all things used as capital to get the next publishing deal. The timing may have been wrong for such a dark-themed book, coming out of years of Covid. I didn't sanitise the experience of depression and some felt that I should have offered more hope of redemption. And yet, I am fiercely, ferociously proud of *Wunderland*, as if its my slightly awkward, ill-behaved middle child who doesn't come across well in public. It felt important to write about depression from a partner's perspective, and in the years since publication, I've had emails from friends, acquaintances and strangers who have experienced (by proxy) similar extremes of depression. The depiction of the helpless rage felt by loved ones was the thing that appealed to them: the bit that offended some reviewers was a comfort to readers with lived experience. That's worth anything. Awards and prizes are incredible but, to hear that the words I've written have connected with another human is the best feeling. Given the internal tussles I had with it, I don't think I could write *Wunderland* again, but I'm glad it exists, satisfied I got through several life changes to pull it out one word at a time.

Wunderland may have been the wrong book by the wrong author at the wrong time, or it may just not have been good enough. But it remains the book of which I'm proudest.

A month after *Wunderland*'s publication, I find myself forgetting it has been published. I'm in the cleaning loop and the parenting loop, uncertain how to get myself back into the writing loop when I hadn't laid firm feet in it to start with. I go to buy some books one day in an independent bookshop in Dublin. The bookseller is very supportive of my writing – I was here signing copies months previously – and before

I can stop her, she brings all the copies of *Wunderland* from the display stand and shelves to the counter for me to sign. I open the first book and see my signed name, the second is the same; all of them are already signed, they haven't sold at all.

I get an Arts Council bursary to be drawn down over two years. (I love the phrase drawn down, old-fashioned ledger words that makes the money seem so real and not hypothetical.) I get urges to ask for it all upfront in hard wads of cash to be sure it won't just disappear into the cloud or be vanquished by a change in government. I squint at the screen, relief at a salary offered, more months of childcare covered. I've earned so little from royalties but so much from bursaries and fellowships to write, chunks of money graciously gifted that translate into time.

Soon after, my son gets sick with Respiratory Syncytial Virus (RSV). My parents offer help but I can't risk infecting them so my partner cycles the child in to me as I finish work if he's in the office, or I race home to take over if he's working from home. I get sick too. I take my last sick day from work and struggle through the rest. I spend the days sitting under a small warm boy in pyjamas. There's nowhere I'd rather be; there are manywheres I should be: Christmas shopping, preparing, writing, a friend's wedding.

In the midst of this, I forget to reply to an important email about a trip overseas, (understandably) piss off the organiser and almost lose the trip, on which I was planning to bring my family. I feel utterly deflated. I can't do all this, I just can't. I'm racing to work, racing home to be with a sick child, getting sick myself. Writing work, and the admin of writing work is falling aside while I prioritise my cleaning job over my family and my writing. Which is the real work here? I need the money, I need some kind of financial security but I don't have the wherewithal to do it all. I am pushing, pushing, pushing and getting nowhere. I was supposed to hand a proposal of this book to my agent and I find myself emailing her to say, yet again, I have a sick child and I can't get to it. Some festive bells fall off the sleigh, I scrawl a few cards, buy the necessary presents online, but Christmas will have to be just so this year. I'm fed-up hearing myself tell yet another person I cancel on / owe an email / essay / phone call to that one kid / two kids / me and the kids have been sick and things have fallen by the wayside. These years I feel like the White Rabbit in *Alice in Wonderland*, scurrying about glancing at my watch shouting I'm late, I'm late, but never quite getting there.

I go into work on the Friday of this very long week feeling wretched. The building that once seemed so beautiful and mysterious now feels dark and bitterly cold. It's minus two outside, I have 110 freezing minutes of coughing and cleaning before the heat comes on. I sit in a library with a sheet of paper and pen and do the maths of whether I can afford some time off with the Arts Council money. I've left the house at 5.25 a.m. too many times to the sounds of a child crying for Mammy. Later that morning, an attendant asks me to do a deep clean of a small locked office I have no key for. The attendant says she has to supervise me for security reasons, that is, presumably, in case I rob a heavy iron safe the size of a washing machine, no matter that I've cleaned this area for five years and have surely proven my honesty. It makes my decision for me: I apply for unpaid leave.

When I open the email stating that my leave has been approved, I am awash with relief. I feel gleeful at the possibilities: time and energy for playing with my children, writing unexhausted. Waking with one or both children squashed onto my face or nestled into my neck in the morning is sheer bliss. Not being beeped awake and having to extricate myself from their small limbs to sneak into my clothes and out the door is a piece of heaven that's hard to describe. Both children bolt up out of sleep and are instantly the widest of awake with roaring joy, ready to pick up where play left off last night. I love being there for the wild energy and manic excitement. And I love being able to collect them from Montessori and have energy to play at their pace. And, to be able to write in the mornings without dragging my brain to the task. And that's where this book really began. It began right here in a grant-funded career break from work.

I've laid out this period of my life chronologically, but so many things from this period are not included that I hesitate to call this a memoir, which suggests something more comprehensive. I mention certain people because of their relevance to my writing story; there are friends and close family members who don't make it onto the pages but who were and are hugely important to me. My partner doesn't feature in this book as an equal parent because I focus on the interaction of my parenting with my writing work, but to not give him equal print-space might inaccurately imply he's not pulling his weight. Running in the background of this whole story is his financial input too: if he didn't work full-time in a stable job, none of this would be possible.

Significant stories remain untold in these pages – for instance, my partner's mother dying after a long illness is not described here because it's not my story to tell, but its impact on our family was huge. This book comes at a very particular slant, the how or not-how of writing, so much is omitted. And finally, handing over this manuscript to my publisher felt strange, like giving my accountant a list of annual expenses that includes his fee: it all felt very familiar and inside-ish. But it also felt homely and right.

Sources

Barnes, E. R. (2021), 'Interview with poet Emily Cooper: "I'm obsessed with recording memories and stories"', *Lucy Writers*, 14 September, https://lucywritersplatform.com/2021/09/14/interview-with-poet-emily-cooper-im-obsessed-with-recording-memories-and-stories/

Barry, S. (2002), *Annie Dunne*, Faber & Faber

Berlin, L. (2015), *A Manual for Cleaning Women: Selected Stories*, Picador

Blair, E. (2021), 'Averted Intimacies', *The New York Review of Books*, 29 April

Currey, M. (2013), *Daily Rituals: How Great Minds Make Time, Find Inspiration, and Get to Work*, Picador

Ernaux, A. (2019), *I Remain in Darkness*, Fitzcarraldo Editions

Galeano, E. (2018), *Football in Sun and Shadow*, Penguin Classics

Greenlaw, L. (2021), *Some Answers Without Questions*, Faber & Faber

Larkin, P. (1964), 'Afternoons', *The Whitsun Weddings*, Faber & Faber, https://thepoetryhour.com/poems/afternoons

Light, A. (2008), *Mrs Woolf and the Servants: an Intimate History of Domestic Life in Bloomsbury*, Penguin

McCracken, K. (1990), 'An Attitude of Compassion: Q&A with Medbh McGuckian', *Irish Literary Supplement*, in J.P. Myers, Jr (ed), *Writing Irish: Selected Interviews with Irish Writers from the Irish Literary Supplement* (1999)

Moore, L. (2001), 'The Art of Fiction No. 167', *The Paris Review*, Spring–Summer

O'Hagan, A. (2021), 'Miss Skippit' (a brief obituary of Mary-Kay Wilmers), *London Review of Books*, 18 February

Olsen, T. (2003), *Silences*, First Feminist Press

Acknowledgements

Some of my descriptions of cleaning have appeared in *The Irish Times*, on RTÉ's *Sunday Miscellany* and on a Trinity Long Room Hub blog post. A version of my student memories also appeared in *Trinity Tales: Trinity College Dublin in the 2000s* (The Lilliput Press) edited by Katie Dickson. So much Trinity. My thoughts on juggling various forms of work appeared in the Behind the Headlines series in the Trinity Long Room Hub (more Trinity). And discussions on rejection, failure and success appeared in talks given at the University of Notre Dame, Indiana, and Babes-Bolyai University, Cluj-Napoca, Romania. Much of this book was written at a desk in the Trinity Long Room Hub (Trinity again) as part of a Rooney Writer Fellowship: my thanks to Peter Rooney, Eve Patten, Caitriona Curtis and all at the Hub. And thanks to Mike Cronin, Thea Gillen and Claire McGowan at Boston College in Dublin for your desk-offering generosity. A huge thank you to the cleaners and supervisors, current and retired, in Trinity College's housekeeping department, for your decency and encouragement, especially to Rose Lucey, Ria Morris, Ger O'Ceallaigh and Caroline Quinn.

Thank you to the teachers for your kindness and dedication, in particular Marita Gleeson for the gold stars and ABCs, Bernie Verdon for the inspiring secondary-school shift and Amanda Piesse at university. To my kind and skilled agent Jessica Bullock for her hugely helpful input on the earliest drafts. To Aoife K. Walsh, Djinn von Noorden and Des Doyle at New Island Books: thank you so much for the belief in and hard work on this book.

To my family and friends. I can't single out anyone for fear of forgetting someone, but thank you all: for the encouragement to start writing this book and to keep at it. And lastly, to my parents, for all of it.